Praise for Profit by Publicity

"This book is a winner! From the first page to the last, it provides step-by-step directions on how to generate the level of publicity real estate professionals want or need in order to succeed. This reference guide is full of examples of the news coverage real agents and brokers have received about their activities, services, and expertise, and expert advice on how you can duplicate their success."
Dale Stinton, CEO
National Association of REALTORS®

"In this up-to-the-minute new reference book by communications expert Edward Segal, you'll discover the benefits and advantages that public relations has over advertising, learn how to effectively promote your community activities, and find out how to use publicity to help achieve business success."
Colleen Badagliacco, 2007 President of the California Association of REALTORS®

"*Profit by Publicity* is a must-read book for every real estate professional. Edward Segal's advice and insights will make you an instant expert on how to generate the publicity you need to help ensure your success in a competitive and challenging industry."
William E. Brown, 2007 President-Elect, California Association of REALTORS®

"Edward Segal has written the ultimate how-to reference guide on publicity that all real estate agents and brokers should have on their desks. This is the only book you'll ever need to help create the publicity you want about your real estate business, activities, or expertise."
David Cabot, 2007 President of the San Diego Association of REALTORS®

"Edward Segal knows public relations, and in *Profit by Publicity* he offers practical, easy-to-understand advice on how to obtain positive news coverage for you and your company. Edward draws on a rich background of experience in the field—from press secretary for members of Congress to media relations strategist

for Fortune 500 companies. His book is essential reading for anyone needing improved public relations."
Jim Fabris, CEO
San Francisco Association of REALTORS®

"This is more than a book—it's like having your own on-call consultant you can turn to whenever you need outstanding and dependable publicity advice. From news releases to speeches, you'll find everything you need to know to help put you or your real estate company on the map—and stay there!"
Jerry Matthews, Advisor
Former CEO of the Illinois and Florida Association of REALTORS®

"*Profit by Publicity* is the secret weapon anyone in real estate must have to help get the publicity and recognition they want. PR guru Edward Segal has a hit a home run with a book that is a joy to read and advice that is easy to follow."
Steve Schneiderman, Publisher, Broker Agent Magazine
San Francisco/North Bay Edition

"Edward Segal shares the secrets to his success in working with the media and generating thousands of stories about hundreds of corporations and organizations. This book shows real estate agents and brokers how to learn from his success and help generate publicity about their own expertise, activities, and accomplishments."
Chip Ahlswede, 2007 Chair, National Association of REALTORS® Government Affairs Directors Committee

"Edward Segal does it again with this insightful new book. His PR expertise becomes your PR expertise as you wend your way though the pages he has written. I recommend both the book and the idea of you becoming a PR expert."
Jay Conrad Levinson
The Father of Guerrilla Marketing
Author, "Guerrilla Marketing" series of books

Profit by Publicity

Profit by Publicity

The How-to Reference Guide for Real Estate Agents and Brokers

Edward Segal

iUniverse, Inc.
New York Lincoln Shanghai

Profit by Publicity
The How-to Reference Guide for Real Estate Agents and Brokers

iUniverse books may be ordered through booksellers or by contacting:

iUniverse
2021 Pine Lake Road, Suite 100
Lincoln, NE 68512
www.iuniverse.com
1-800-Authors (1-800-288-4677)

ISBN-13: 978-0-595-42509-9
ISBN-10: 0-595-42509-7

Printed in the United States of America

To my friends and colleagues at the Marin Association of
REALTORS®—the adventure continues!

Acknowledgements

Writing this book was a solitary task, but preparing the manuscript for publication was a team effort.

I want to thank the following leaders and members of the Marin Association of REALTORS® for taking time out of their busy professional lives to review the draft manuscript and offer their valuable insights, perspectives, and recommendations: Kathy Schlegel, Jack Wilkinson, Kay Moore, Valerie Castellana, Kate Hamilton, Roberta DiPrete, Jack McLaughlin, Kevin Pastel, Katie Beacock, Barry Crotty, Kathleen Hilken, John Zeiter, Steve Dickason, John Truong, Arundel Burrell, and Levi Swift.

Their thoughtful comments helped ensure that this book will meet and exceed the expectations of their colleagues in the real estate profession.

My grateful appreciation goes to Nancy Kervin for her research and proofreading skill, and amazing ability to find needles in haystacks; to Arnold Sanow for his moral support; to my literary agent, Michael Larsen, for his diligent efforts and wise counsel over the years; and to Caren Callahan for her legal prowess.

Last but certainly not least, I want to thank my wife, Pamela Segal. Her advice and counsel helps make me a better writer and helped make this a better book.

Contents

Take Stock of Your Real Estate Expertise and Services

To help you prepare a publicity plan for you or your company, it's important to ask yourself 15 key questions. The answers will help identify and prioritize which aspects of a real estate agent's business activities or professional life may be worthy of publicity, what they want to be known for, and how much publicity they want.

If It Works for Coke and Disney, It Will Work for You

Shows why it is important for real estate agents to develop a personal brand that will help people and the media sit up and take notice and make it easier to achieve the visibility they want.

How to Hit the Publicity Bull's-eye

Explains how to define, identify, and target the audiences who will be most interested in watching real estate agents on television, reading about them in newspapers and magazines, and listening to them on radio.

Once Upon a Time ...

News organizations, which are a gateway between individuals and publicity, are storytellers who tell their stories to readers, viewers, and listeners. This chapter explains why real estate agents and brokers should be their own storyteller.

Do You Have Any Idea What You're Talking About?

Credibility and expertise are two key ingredients in the efforts by real estate agents to generate publicity. This chapter talks about the importance of research to help bolster your claims, prove your points, and strengthen your arguments.

This chapter shows how real estate professionals can ensure that stories are reported the way they want by limiting, summarizing, and prioritizing the information they provide to news organizations.

This chapter discusses the best ways to convince journalists to do stories about you or your company; includes a list of more than two dozen proven story hooks and news angles.

Unless you can show your story, you will only communicate half your story to the media and target audience. This chapter explains why pictures are important to television, newspapers, and even radio, and how effective visuals can help attract the attention of editors and reporters.

Explains why you need a written plan to generate publicity and includes a worksheet to help prepare it.

This chapter shows how by test-marketing their plan, real estate agents can help ensure it will work; explains why testing will help make the plan stronger and more effective.

If real estate agents don't have the time, talent, or energy to generate publicity on their own, they can use a PR agency or consultant.

What Your Mother Never Told You about Publicity

                    It May be English to You, But It's All Greek to Them

                    Many people assume that anyone who speaks English
                    should automatically understand the references, allusions,
                    or comparisons they make to popular culture or history.
                    Find out why this is not always the case.

                    Speechless in Seattle (or Anywhere Else)

                    What should you do if you come down with a severe case of
                    stage fright when asked to give a speech? Arnold Sanow,
                    who overcame his fear of speaking in public to become a
                    professional speaker, shares his secrets for success. This
                    chapter includes a checklist of items to keep in mind to help
                    ensure you deliver successful presentations.

                    3 ... 2 ... 1

                    Timing is an important factor in determining whether and
                    how much publicity a real estate agent can generate. This
                    chapter explains the best months of the year, days of the
                    week, and times of the day for attracting the attention of the
                    general public and the media.

                    But Don't Go Overboard

                    How real estate agents present themselves to the world helps
                    shape how they are perceived by the public. This chapter
                    shows some of the worst ways others have tried to capture
                    the public's attention.

                    They Don't Have Horns or Eat Their Young

                    Discusses the 19 best ways to understand and work with
                    editors and reporters, and which strategies and tactics are

Your Checklist for Interview Success

This chapter lists 64 ways to help guarantee that the interviews you do with reporters are productive and successful, to ensure your quotes are more likely to be used by journalists in their stories, and to make sure that the media does an accurate job of reporting.

The Magic Seven Seconds

Unless you can summarize your story in seven seconds or less, your quotes will be left on the cutting room floor; this chapter lists guidelines to prepare sound and ink bites so reporters will be more likely to include them in their stories.

Don't Be a Victim of Murphy's Law

The chapter explains 15 things that can go wrong when real estate agents deal with the media and the steps agents and brokers can take to ensure their stories are read, seen, or heard by the public.

Don't Take It Laying Down

This chapter looks at the 15 most common reporting mistakes and four ways to correct them.

It's Not Who You Know, but Who Knows about You

Five steps you can take to ensure that reporters know about and can contact you for interviews.

This chapter explains how to use news outlets as a continuing education class about the media and how to take advantage of that knowledge.

News organizations across the country have their own problems to contend with as they try to do the best job they can to report the news. This chapter examines 11 of those problems and suggests five ways to exploit those problems to ensure news coverage about you or your real estate company.

Discusses how newspapers differ from other types of news organizations, and how agents and brokers should conduct themselves during interviews.

This chapter includes advice on how to do interviews on television news shows, including a list of 12 things real estate agents should do to get the most out of their interviews.

This chapter discusses the best ways to act during live or taped radio interviews. Also includes a helpful checklist of nine things real estate agents should do before, during, and after interviews.

A Special Invitation

This chapter outlines the nine ingredients of news advisories that can help get reporters interested in doing stories about the events or activities of your real estate company.

I Was Born in a Log Cabin...

This chapter provides examples of the different kinds of profile stories that news organizations might do about you, the two ways in which most profile stories are alike, and the secret for getting a news outlet to profile you or your company.

Everyone is Entitled to My Opinion

Nine ways to prepare opinion pieces to ensure they are published in newspapers.

Dear Sir:

Eight ways to help guarantee your letters to newspapers or magazines are published.

Lights, Camera, Action!

How you can generate national publicity by packaging and distributing a self-produced television story.

Risks and Rewards

The benefits and drawbacks of staging a news conference, and 14 steps you can take to ensure their success.

How to be in Two Places at Once

Practical advice on when and why you may want to use satellite technology to help spread the word about yourself or your company.

Introduction

Profit by Publicity is based on my experience in public relations, journalism, politics, and the real estate profession. This book is organized so you can use it as a how-to reference guide to hundreds of proven and effective tips, tools, and solutions to help generate publicity about yourself or your real estate company—publicity that can provide a competitive edge in the marketplace.

No matter how long you've been in real estate, where you work, or who you work for, this book will show you:

- How to publicize your services, expertise, activities, and accomplishments.

- The activities and projects television stations, newspapers, and other news organizations are most interested in covering and the story angles and news hooks you can use to help convince reporters to do stories about you or your company. As you read the following pages, you may realize you are already implementing one or more of these newsworthy activities *but never thought to generate publicity about them.*

- How to prepare effective press materials, including news releases, press kits, biographical profiles, and news advisories. For the latest examples of these and other materials, go to www.ProfitByPublicity.com and click on the link to "tools of the trade". Also, be sure to visit my blog at http://ProfitByPublicity.blogspot.com.

- How to get the most out of your publicity.

The examples in this book are based largely on the successes of real estate agents, brokers, real estate companies, and REALTOR® associations across the country that have already generated publicity about themselves. But I've also included a handful of examples from outside the real estate industry of people who have made embarrassing PR mistakes or lapses in judgment. Obviously, you'll want to duplicate the successes and avoid the mistakes.

Unless otherwise noted, the publicity examples are excerpted from daily and weekly newspapers across the country.

While most of the excerpts are about real estate professionals, the news hooks and story angles on which the articles are based will work just as well for REALTOR® associations or other real estate-related organizations and businesses.

In "Is It Time to Start Bragging About Yourself?," *Fortune* magazine noted that, "there's nothing like a little positive press to promote yourself ... the bottom line is that most publicity is good publicity." The magazine warned, however, that "if you are ready to take the plunge and enter the bracing work of self-promotion, you ought to find the right way to go about it. "

I wrote this book to help you do just that.

Credentials

My background includes serving as:

- Chief executive officer and communications director of the Marin Association of REALTORS®, where I've generated hundreds of stories in the local, state, national, and international media about the activities and accomplishments of the California-based organization.

- The marketing strategies columnist for *The Wall Street Journal's* StartupJournal.com

- A PR consultant to more than 500 clients, including Ford Motor Company, Marriott Corporation, E-Myth Worldwide, Air Travelers Association, Society of the Plastics Industry, clients of Ogilvy Public Relations Worldwide, and the Society of Manufacturing Engineers.

- A freelance writer whose work has appeared in the *Washington Post, The New York Times, The Wall Street Journal, Los Angeles Times,* and other publications.

- An instructor at San Jose State University's professional development program, teaching classes on media interview techniques; I've taught similar courses at the Learning Annex and First Class adult education centers.

- A media trainer and presentation skills coach who conducts workshops for the National Association of REALTORS®, the California Association of REALTORS® and leaders of the Marin Association of REALTORS®, local REALTOR® associations, and real estate brokers.

- Press secretary to members of Congress on Capitol Hill and aide to presidential and congressional candidates.

Profit by Publicity illustrates and discusses many different ways to use public relations activities as part of your ongoing marketing efforts. Only you can decide which of the strategies and tactics are a good fit for you or your company; make sense within the framework of your own business or marketing plans; and are appropriate given the time, money, and resources you'll want to devote to these efforts.

One Last Thing

Some final words before we get started:

- The National Association of REALTORS® (NAR) requires that the word "REALTOR®" be in all capitalized letters and include a registration mark. While I follow this rule for the copy I wrote for the book, most news organizations do not adhere to this protocol in their stories. Therefore, I've left the word unchanged from the way it originally appeared in their stories.

- NAR has strict guidelines for the proper use of the REALTOR® name and logo, and requires people to follow those guidelines when using the REALTOR® name and logo in their press and marketing materials. For more information, go to www.realtors.org.

- As appropriate, I've included in some chapters resource information about vendors or services you may want to consider to help implement your public relations activities. While I may have used some of them in the past, I do not endorse them or guarantee their information, services, fees, prices, or performance. You should evaluate each of them on their own merits, request and review their costs or estimates and decide for yourself whether to use them.

- To ensure you receive the help you need from these resources, it is important that you be as specific and detailed as possible with them about the type or level of assistance you are seeking and the kind of information you are after.

- When dealing with consultants or PR firms, there are no such things as stupid questions or too many questions, so be sure you find out as much as you need to know before you make a decision about their services or fees.

Part I

Prepare Your Roadmap

*If You Don't Know Where You're Going,
You'll Never Know if You Get There*

Chapter 1

The Benefits and Advantages of Publicity

What's In It for You

The benefits and advantages of publicity, and how it has helped real estate professionals establish their reputation, generate more leads, obtain more listings, and sell more properties.

Pat Thatcher-Hill, ABR, GRI, SRS, is a REALTOR® with Real Estate Associates of Falmouth in Falmouth, Mass. "The market visibility I [now] have is such that I'm one of the first agents people think of to call or represent them," she says. Thatcher credits her success in generating leads, listings, and sales to the visibility created by news releases she distributes about her business activities, real estate education, and community involvement.

Robin Diessner is the owner/broker of Intero Real Estate in Arizona. She has been interviewed and profiled by scores of local, state, and national news organizations, ranging from television stations to *The Wall Street Journal*. Diessner says the news coverage has "had a huge impact" on her business by helping establish the firm in the marketplace, creating a good reputation for the company, and attracting agents to work for her.

Staci Dancey, a REALTOR® broker with Century 21 Masters in Orange, Calif., was quoted in news reports about placing a listing price on the White House if it were to go on the market. An attorney with the U.S. Department of Justice later read her comments and invited her to compete to represent a foreclosure property in Newport Beach, Calif. Dancey was eventually selected to sell the $2.1 million residence and received a $115,000 commission for listing the home and finding a buyer. Dancey credits the publicity she received about her comments for making it possible to compete for the lucrative listing in the first place.

Steven Good is a Chicago-based REALTOR® and former president of the Chicago Association of REALTORS®. He has written articles on various aspects of real estate which have appeared in dozens of magazines and other publications. Good says almost all of his company's business comes from the visibility he and his firm, Sheldon Good & Company, receive from these and other public relations activities.

Sperry Van Ness is a national commercial real estate brokerage headquartered in Irvine, Calif. Company officials credit press coverage for helping Sperry Van Ness generate a seven-fold increase in sales volume between 2001 and 2006. Officials say they rely heavily on publicity to help promote and market the company, and now generate almost 200 stories a month about the company's expertise and accomplishments.

These real estate agents, brokers, and companies have learned two important marketing lessons:

1. Like advertising, frequency matters: the more people hear or read about you in the media or hear your speeches and presentations, the more likely it is they will use your services.

2. The more impact you can make with your public relations activities, the more likely it is people will know and remember you.

Thatcher-Hill, Diessner, Dancey, Good, and Sperry Van Ness are hardly alone in knowing the value and importance of public relations.

As the Web site of the National Association of REALTORS® observes, "… public relations is a no-cost/low-cost personal marketing option that can bring you a substantial increase in your business profile—and your profits."

But public relations remains a rarely used marketing tool by the nation's four million real estate agents and brokers. Why? As marketing guru Arnie Sanow, author of *Get Along with Anyone, Anytime, Anywhere*, notes, "Real estate professionals know how to promote property, but usually have no idea how to publicize themselves. Most real estate agents and brokers simply don't know about or how to use proven public relations tools, tips, and solutions to market themselves."

This book will show you how to understand and do just that.

The Bottom Line

- Publicity has helped agents and brokers succeed in real estate.
- The more publicity you generate, the more impact it will have.
- Publicity is a rarely used, but affordable, tool for real estate professionals.

How to Generate Publicity: Launch a New Service

House Won't Sell? Have a Cow, Man

Although there may always be sign-waving clowns and cookies baking in the oven, the Internet is playing a bigger role in how the industry interacts with clients and prospective home buyers. Coldwell Banker Real Estate Corp., for example, parent company of Florida's largest residential real-estate agency, recently launched an online service that allows potential customers to receive personalized listings and daily mortgage updates.

The company also allows would-be home buyers to type questions on its Florida-specific Web site, floridamoves.com, which automatically generates voice mails for a quick response from a nearby agent.

Orlando Sentinel
Nov. 4, 2006
Orlando, Fla.

Advice and Insights: Necessity is the mother of invention—and can be the inspiration for new services to meet the challenges of a changing market and the needs of consumers. Thanks to the Internet, it's easier than ever before to launch and implement services based on your knowledge, expertise, or existing resources.

No matter whether your new service is high-tech or no-tech, check to ensure it is truly different or better than what your competition is offering, that you have proper credentials, expertise, or background to provide the service, and that you have the resources to meet the demand for it.

And be sure the new service works before distributing a news release about it, or the publicity you receive might not be the publicity you want.

Chapter 2

The Difference Between Advertising and Publicity

Why Not Just Buy an Ad?

Some people think the best way to get publicity is buy an ad in the paper or a commercial on television. Here's why they're wrong.

At the seminars and workshops I conduct across the country, real estate agents often ask me why they can't simply buy the exposure they want by purchasing advertising. They want to know what difference it makes whether their public recognition comes from commercials or news coverage.

The difference is crucial and can be summarized in one word: *credibility.*

- If you have enough money, you can buy any amount of advertising, have it say whatever you want, and have it appear almost anywhere or anytime you want for as long as you like. But it is impossible to buy favorable news coverage for you or your company in the daily newspaper, or charge a human-interest story on the evening news of a local television station to your credit card.

- Knowing that you could not possibly have paid off a news organization to run a story, the public will place more credibility in an objective news account about you than if you had said the same thing in a full-page ad or 30-second commercial.

For many corporations, publicity can be more important than commercials.

Debra Leopold is the founder of First Class, Inc., an independently owned non-profit continuing education center in Washington, D.C. She says: "I could spend thousands of dollars on a full-page newspaper ad and still not get the name response I've received by simply buying a postage stamp and sending out a news release. News releases have more credibility than advertising. I've abandoned all of my advertising efforts and now concentrate entirely on public relations. I simply cannot get the same response with an ad as I can with a one- or two-line mention in a newspaper story."

A survey of 3,000 company managers conducted by Erdos & Morgan for the American Advertising Federation found that corporate America placed more importance on public relations than advertising. Asked about the "strategic importance" of seven different departments that can help companies meet their marketing and sales goals, public relations came in third, just after product development and strategic marketing. Advertising was rated sixth.

The Bottom Line

- Publicity has more credibility than advertising.
- You can buy ads, but you can't buy a good story in the media.
- Many corporations and organizations prefer public relations over advertising to help market themselves.

How to Generate Publicity: Raise Money for a Good Cause

Local Realtor Hosts 'Home In On a Cure' Fundraiser
Lending a hand to help to combat neuromuscular disease, ERA Mata Realty will host "Home in on a Cure" Wine and Beer Tasting fundraising event at the Erwin Meier Administration Building, 625 Court St., Woodland. "For the past 30 years, ERA Real Estate has been the sole corporate sponsor of the Muscular Dystrophy Association from the real estate industry. We're proud of the work we have done to support this great cause, including raising $30 million since 1977 to help MDA in the fight against neuromuscular diseases," said Broker David Mata.

Daily Democrat
Nov. 4, 2006
Woodland, Calif.

Advice and Insights: Raising money to help pay for worthwhile community projects or activities can be made that much easier by seeking public support through news stories about your efforts. And, for the real estate agents or brokers who play a role in raising those funds, news coverage about their generosity can help their own public image, positioning them as good corporate citizens who want to give something back to their neighborhood.

It's one thing for a corporation such as ERA Real Estate to raise $10 million, but it would be quite an accomplishment for a single broker or agent to do the same. That's why, in most cases, collecting hundreds of thousands of dollars for a local charity is usually all that is takes to merit a mention by the media. Sometimes, though, it's not how much you raise, but how you try to raise it, that can generate publicity. For example:

Real Charitable: Brokers Donate 15% of Commissions to Charity
[Erica] Laughlin has pledged 15 percent of her gross commissions to charity since she started Foundation Realty last year. She has since become friends and established an informal business relationship with Lori Nitzel, who also started her firm, Full Circle Realty, last year with a pledge to donate 15 percent of his gross commissions to charity.

The Capital Times
June 29, 2006
Madison, Wis.

Chapter 3

Your Opportunities for Publicity

It's a Jungle Out There!

The chapter explains why real estate agents have a wealth of opportunities for publicity, and discusses the competition they'll face from others who want to be or are already well known.

News organizations are the most important stepping stones to publicity in our society. That's because television stations, radio stations, newsletters, Web sites, blogs, podcasts, magazines, and newspapers are among the most effective ways for individuals, companies, and organizations to communicate with the rest of society.

Many news outlets have their own staff of editors, reporters, commentators, or columnists; a defined audience; a list of topics or subjects they follow; their own definition of news; and schedules for when they produce and distribute their product to their viewers, listeners, or readers.

They also have a tremendous vacuum to fill every day, week, or month in finding and providing enough information to fill hundreds of thousands of hours of airtime and millions of pages of print *every year* with news and information.

The challenge these news organizations have in finding and providing news to their audiences also represents an important opportunity for you—*if* you are able to present your real estate expertise, activities, opinions, or accomplishments as news. If you can, then you may have an excellent chance to convince news outlets to do a story about you or your real estate company.

First the Bad News

The bad news is that you're bound to face some degree of competition in your efforts to capture the attention of the media. That competition may come from:

- Other real estate agents or brokers.

- Hundreds of corporations and organizations that have full-time staff or entire departments devoted to publicizing or promoting their products and services.

- Thousands of public relations and marketing consultants and agencies that are seeking to generate news coverage for or about their clients.

- Current events and late-breaking stories that compete for the limited "news hole" that news organizations are able to fill every day.

Now for the Good News

Fortunately, real estate agents and brokers can take steps to ensure they are on a level playing field and have the same opportunity for publicity as their competition. That's because every individual, corporation, or organization who seeks publicity, including you, has to provide the answers to two key questions in order to help convince reporters to do a story:

Those questions are: who cares and why.

Specifically:

- *Who cares* what you have to say, the story you have to tell, or your real estate services or expertise?

- *Why* should they care in the first place?

How you answer these pivotal questions—combined with your ability to conduct successful interviews with editors and reporters who are interested in doing stories about you or your company—will help determine whether and how you will stand out against your competition, and how much publicity you or your company will receive. Once you've identified and prioritized what you want to be known for (see Chapter 5), you should define, identify, and target the audiences who will be most interested to watch, read, or hear stories about it.

Using this worksheet, a blank sheet of paper, or a computer screen, answer the following questions about the top priority for which you want to be known. (Sample answers are in italics.)

1. Based on your own marketing or other reasons, which target audiences will be the most important ones to learn about you or your company? *First-time home buyers.*

2. Why will they be interested to learn about you or your company? *Because I have a proven track record of selling homes to first-time home buyers.*

3. Which groups and organizations do members of your target audience belong to? *Single clubs and church groups.*

4. Where do they live? *Out of town and in apartment complexes in the downtown area.*

5. What demographic information is available about your target audience that may help you to target and understand them? *Mostly college educated women in their 20s and 30s.*

In the pages that follow, I'll discuss the steps you can take to show reporters why they should do stories about you and the most effective ways to deal with the media.

The Bottom Line

- News organizations are the gateway to publicity.
- News outlets have a never-ending need for content.
- Real estate professionals can help fill this need—and generate publicity for themselves—if they present their activities and accomplishments as news.
- Manage your expectations about how much publicity you can expect to generate.
- Identify and define your audience before you seek to generate publicity about yourself or your real estate company.
- Once you know who your audience is, seek to obtain as much information about them as possible.
- The more you know your audience, the more effectively you will be able to tell your story to them.

How to Generate Publicity: Discuss Marketing Tactics

Realtors Vary in Their Opinions about Showing Properties Up For Sale
For Hope Callihan, broker associate and co-owner of A Home Town Realty in Haines City, the open house definitely is a thing of the past, the long past. "It's a dinosaur," Callihan said. "It's pretty much extinct. It hasn't worked for us for the past three or four years."

The Ledger
June 4, 2005
Lakeland, Fla.

Advice and Insights: Reporters who cover real estate and business topics for their news organizations often turn to local agents and brokers for comments and observations about the latest trends and developments in residential and commercial real estate. Your ability to become a source of information to the media can depend on the following three factors:

1. Can you boil down your comments to a few words? (See Chapter 22)

2. Do you have the credentials and expertise to talk about the topic? (See Chapters 5)

3. Can you convince a reporter why you should be interviewed? (See Chapter 11)

Chapter 4

Publicity on a Shoestring

You Don't Have to Be Rich to Generate News Coverage

Dispels the myth that real estate agents need a lot of money to generate publicity, and shows how much money is really necessary to become widely recognized.

One of the biggest misconceptions many real estate agents and brokers have about publicity is that it takes many thousands of dollars to generate news coverage about their services, expertise, or accomplishments.

The reality is that most public relations activities don't have to cost you anything more than your creativity, time, price of a postage stamp or the effort it takes to call a reporter, send a fax, or send an e-mail message.

How much money and time it will take *you* will depend on:

1. The effort necessary to prepare your story so it can be told effectively and convincingly to editors and reporters.

2. How much research you will need to do to obtain the facts, figures, or other information necessary to tell your story to the media. (See Chapter 9)

3. The "tools of the trade" you'll need to tell or show your story, such as news releases, press kits, photographs, video news releases, etc. (See part IV)

4. Whether you decide to hire a public relations consultant or agency. (See Chapter 15)

The Bottom Line

- You don't need a lot of money to generate a lot of publicity.
- Several factors will impact on how money you may need to spend.

How to Generate Publicity: Set Yourself Apart from the Competition

Practitioners Try Folksy, First-Name Style
Real estate practitioners are dropping last names from their "for sale" signs to set themselves apart from a sea of competition. Ken Kuhl and Don Barrett, who have been working as a team at William Raveis since 1997, in Hartford, Conn., said marketing themselves as Ken and Don seemed natural because that's how people already know them in the community. "To a large extent we have become known by our first names. It's almost like branding our team," Kuhl said.

Hartford Courant
Feb. 16, 2005
Hartford, Conn.

Advice and Insights: Sometimes it's the little things you can do that can trigger the publicity you want. Something as simple as dropping your last name from for sale signs could be enough to merit a story in your local paper. The tactic certainly worked for these agents.

Chapter 5

Decide Who or What You Want to Publicize

Take Stock of Your Real Estate Expertise and Services

To help you prepare a publicity plan for you or your company, it's important to ask yourself 15 key questions. The answers will help identify and prioritize which aspects of a real estate agent's business activities or professional life may be worthy of publicity, what they want to be known for, and how much publicity they want.

Whether you want to generate publicity about your real estate expertise, give an occasional speech, or get more involved in community groups and organizations, there are some basic questions you should ask yourself before you plan or implement any public relations activities.

The answers will help guide the nature and direction of your public relations activities.

Who or what do I want to publicize?

- Myself
- My company

What aspect of my real estate expertise do I want to publicize?

- Knowledge of local market conditions
- Real estate trends or predictions
- Home buyers
- Home sellers
- Second homes

- Resorts
- Vacation homes
- Rentals
- Land
- Condominiums
- Commercial investment properties
- Property management
- Baby boomers
- Seniors
- Ethnic or non-English speaking buyers
- Other _____

Who is my target audience?
- Potential home buyers
- Investors
- Potential home sellers
- Friends
- Neighbors
- Peers
- Past clients

What is my geographic focus?
- Selected neighborhoods or communities
- A targeted town or city
- Metropolitan area or region
- Statewide
- National
- International

Which news organizations are in that area I will focus on?
- Weekly newspapers
- Daily newspapers
- Magazines

- Radio stations
- Television stations

Which groups and organizations are in this area?

- Chambers of commerce
- PTAs
- Homeowners associations
- Service groups and organizations (Kiwanis, Lions Club, etc.)
- Others _____

Which ones do I belong to or can I join?

- _____
- _____
- _____
- _____
- _____

How many other real estate agents or brokers will I be competing against for publicity in my area?

- Up to 50
- Up to 100
- Up to 500
- Up to 1,000
- Up to 5,000
- Up to 10,000
- Up to 20,000
- More than 20,000

How much publicity do I want?

- To be recognized in my neighborhood, city, county, or state
- To become a household word in the real estate industry
- To be as well known to the general public as Donald Trump

What degree of public recognition am I seeking?

- Newspaper and magazine profile stories in which I am the star attraction
- To be quoted within the body of a newspaper or magazine article
- To appear on television or radio news programs with analysis and observations of the housing market
- Other _____

What PR-related skills do I have?

- Writing
- Public speaking
- Pitching story ideas to editors and reporters
- Thinking on my feet
- Networking
- Other _____

Who do I have to help me with my marketing efforts?

- No one
- Friends and family members
- Colleagues
- My office staff
- A public relations consultant or agency
- Other _____

How much time will I be able to set aside every month to publicize myself?

- *None*
- *1 to 5 hours*
- *5 to 10 hours*
- *10 to 15 hours*
- *15 to 20 hours*
- *More than 20 hours*

What resources do I have access to for real estate-related information and research?

- My local or regional multiple listing service
- My company or broker

- My local association of REALTORS®
- My state association of REALTORS®
- The National Association of REALTORS®
- Local library
- The Internet
- Local college or university
- Other _____

How much am I prepared to spend on my public relations activities?
- Nothing
- As little as possible
- Up to $500
- Up to $1,000
- Up to $5,000
- Up to $10,000
- More than $10,000

If you want to spend nothing or as little as possible, then you'll like what I have to say in Chapter 4 about publicity budgets. If you want to get as much bang for the bucks that you are willing to spend, you'll want to read it as well.

The Bottom Line

- Before you try to generate publicity about yourself or real estate company, there are several important questions you must ask yourself about your business, competition, publicity goals, target audiences, and available resources.
- Your honest answers will help you to prepare a realistic publicity plan.

How to Generate Publicity: Attend Workshops

Realtors Attend Training on Brownfields
Cranston Real Estate Realtors Lydia Donnelly, Pamela Hadley, Janet Henry, and Madelyn Heslop attended the Brownfields Site training in Perry County, Ohio on June 7.

Marietta Times
June 9, 2006
Marietta, Ga.

Advice and Insights: Sometimes the best story angles may be the boring ones—such as taking a class. But they may be all you need in order to generate publicity. Be sure to keep your expectations low, however, since the "news" that you took a real estate-related class is not likely to be featured on the front page of your local paper.

Sometimes even attending a seminar sponsored by a real estate company can result in a story. For example:

Realtors Attend Conference
Jewel and Mickey Pendergrass, owners of Century 21 LeMac Realty, attended the national Century 21 Leadership Conference in Rancho Mirage, Calif., recently where they were able to network with other brokers from all over the United States. The theme of the meeting was "Power of Gold," referring to the new Century 21 Property Search Gold, which is Web-based and supplies details about property listings including a map view, satellite view or hybrid view.

The Baxter Bulletin
Mountain Home, Ark.
Nov. 7, 2006

Chapter 6

How to Brand Yourself

If It Works for Coke and Disney, It Will Work for You

Shows why it is important for real estate agents to develop a personal brand that will help people and the media sit up and take notice and make it easier to achieve the visibility they want.

If I held up an unmarked bottle of brown liquid, you'd have no idea what was in it or how it is used. But if I told you that it was a bottle of Coca-Cola, then you'd know exactly what it was and what you could do with it. You'd even have a good idea of what it tastes like.

Such is the power of branding, which can immediately communicate the benefits and advantages of a product or company through the use of a name, logo, symbol, or phrase.

If branding works for Coca-Cola, Google, Walt Disney Company, and thousands of other companies and organizations, then it can certainly work for you to help quickly communicate who you are, what you do, how well you do it, etc.

Another example of effective branding is the campaign by the National Association of REALTORS® to publicize the benefits and advantages to the public of working with members of local REALTOR® associations.

NAR has spent millions of dollars in advertising to promote the professionalism and code of ethics of REALTORS®, and encourages its members to use the REALTOR® title and logo in all their marketing materials.

Deciding what you'd like your reputation or brand to represent will take some careful consideration on your part.

When people hear your name, see your picture or look at your business card, what words or image do you want them to associate with you?

One real estate agency sought to generate publicity by announcing its expansion plans and brand identity in a news release distributed on BusinessWire:

SOUTHBURY, Conn.—Casa Latino Real Estate, which began operations in 2005 as a single real estate agency in Connecticut, is about to make history. By this time next year, it is expected that Casa Latino Real Estate offices will be found in cities and towns from coast to coast, and will be the first and only nationally recognized Hispanic real estate brand.

BusinessWire
Aug. 11, 2006

Whatever "brand" you select should be communicated in all that you do and say about your real estate business. But you must ensure that your image or reputation is consistent and reflects the real you, and can be justified and substantiated. Otherwise, the brand people will start to associate with you is that of "phony", "fraud", or "fake."

Resources

For information on NAR's branding campaign, please visit www.realtors.org.

Exercise: What's Your Brand?

This exercise will help you begin the task of identifying and selecting a brand identity for you or your real estate company.

Brands are too important to leave in the hands of one individual. If you own a real estate company, it's important that you consult with all members of your leadership team in deciding and adopting your corporate brand. If you are an individual real estate agent, seek feedback from your friends, family, neighbors, and colleagues.

But this exercise can help you get started in the right direction.

1. On the left side of the page, list all the characteristics you'd like your target audience to know, understand, or believe about you or your company.

   Examples include knowing how to use various hardware and software to help your client, taking extra training to improve your professional skills, and a proven ability to sell property.

2. On the right side of the page, jot down the word or phrase that best describes each of the characteristics you listed on the left side of the page. *Examples include "tech savvy," "top-producer," and "professional."*

Characteristics   **Short Description**

_____

_____

_____

_____

3. In the space below, list your services, expertise, activities, or accomplishments that support the information you just listed. *Examples include selling 20 homes last year, earning appropriate designations from the National Association of REALTORS®, etc.*

_____

_____

_____

_____

4. Finally, go back through the list above and prioritize the "brand identities" that best represent you or your company and are best supported by your services, expertise, or activities. Which ones do you feel most comfortable with, and for which you'd like to be known? *For example, specializing in helping people who are trying to buy their first home*

_____

_____

_____

_____

_____

The results of this exercise might look something like this:
"I am a tech-savvy, top-producing real estate agent specializing in first-time home buyers in the Arlington, Virginia area. I have received several professional designations from the National Association of REALTORS® as proof of my professionalism, expertise, and credentials."

The Bottom Line

- You need a brand to help distinguish yourself from other real estate agents or brokers.
- Live up to the brand you select.
- Promote your brand in all of your marketing activities and materials.

How to Generate Publicity: Promote Your Professional Designations

Real Estate News for People on the Go
Dan Patterson of RE/MAX Heritage has finished key courses to earn the Certified Residential Specialist designation given by the Council of Residential Specialists, an affiliate of the National Association of Realtors. The course included techniques in seller counseling, pricing, client servicing and marketing techniques.

Pittsburgh Post-Gazette
Oct. 15, 2006
Pittsburgh, Pa.

Advice and Insights: Obtaining one or more professional designations can be an important way to demonstrate how you are different or better than your competition.

Once you've received the designation, don't be shy in telling others about your accomplishment. While a news release announcing your designation will not land you on the front page of the daily newspaper, it could be included as a short news item in the paper's news briefs, business digest, or movers and shakers columns.

In addition to publicizing your designations and what they mean for your clients, be sure to include your designations on the home page of your Web site, on your business cards, and in other marketing materials.

REALTORS® who are interested in obtaining designations through the National Association of REALTORS® should go to www.realtors.org, or contact their local or state REALTOR® association.

Chapter 7

Define, Target, and Find Your Audience

How to Hit the Publicity Bull's-eye

Explains how to define, identify, and target the audiences who will be most interested in watching real estate agents on television, reading about them in newspapers and magazines, and listening to them on radio.

It's important to ask yourself—and prioritize—which aspects of your real estate business you want to publicize, to which target audience, and why. The answers may provide the reason why a news organization would want to do a story about you or your company. An agent in Michigan merited the following newspaper story about her focus on foreclosed properties:

Taped Out
Every Week, Chris Wretschko gets new evidence that foreclosures on home mortgages are on the way up. Wretschko, whose real estate firm, Gateway to Homes in Lansing Township, specializes in foreclosures, figures her listings have doubled since last year. She has 50 foreclosed houses listed currently and adds several more each week.

Lansing State Journal
June 24, 2006
Lansing, Mich.

An inventory of *your* expertise or services should not be prepared in a vacuum, but rather in conjunction with your business plan or existing marketing strategy.

Using this worksheet (or any piece of paper or a blank computer screen):

1. Briefly list and describe the real estate-related services, activities, accomplishments, areas of expertise, or opinions and viewpoints for which you want to be known.

   For example: *The current cooling of the housing market in our area provides important opportunities for baby boomers to buy their second or vacation home.*

2. Explain why you or your company have the qualifications or credibility for a news organization to do a story about you.

   For example: *I have been a real estate agent for ten years, was named REALTOR® of the year by my local association, and have earned more professional designations than 95 percent of the other agents in the tri-county region.*

3. Prioritize each of your services, activities, etc. based on which are most important for you or for which you'd like to be known.

How to Generate Publicity: Start a New Company or Open a New Office

Agents Form New Real Estate Venture
Just in time for Independence Day, a group of local real estate agents have formed Patriot Realty. The group says it will soon establish an office in the Avery Ranch area, a move that will "bring them to the heart of the rapidly expanding northwestern areas of Austin."

Austin Business Journal
July 3, 2006
Austin, Tex.

Advice and Insights: Generating news coverage about the start of a new real estate company can help ensure that potential home buyers and home sellers know that it is or soon will be open for business. And since clients are the lifeblood of any real estate agency, the sooner you get noticed, the better!

Considering the hundreds of thousands of new businesses that are launched every year, you'll need all the help you can get to make sure the public knows your real estate company exists.

Fortunately, local news organizations regard entrepreneurs and their new companies as an important source of stories and articles for their audiences.

To help ensure maximum news coverage, it is important to include the following information in your press materials (for more advice on preparing effective news releases, see Chapter 34):

- A description of the real estate services or expertise you'll offer.
- Any particular benefits or advantages you'll offer to home buyers or sellers.
- When your new agency started or will be open for business.
- Why you started the company in the first place.
- Where it's located.
- Relevant background information about yourself or the broker/owners.
- How many agents will be working in your office.
- How to contact you or the agency for more information.

The more news and information about the new real estate company you can include in the news release, the better. Indeed, a news story about your new company can do more than simply announce the venture—it can also tell people where you're located and demonstrate early momentum for the newly launched business. For example:

Allen Tate Realtors Coming To Town
Allen Tate Realtors, a giant in the North Carolina residential real-estate market, has arrived in Winston-Salem. The company is scheduled to open its first office here on Nov. 22 at the David House at Polo and Reynolds roads.

Winston-Salem Journal
Nov. 4, 2004
Winston-Salem, N.C.

You can get more bang for your publicity buck—and longer stories—by using the opening of a new office to also show momentum for your company. For example:

Two familiar names in Clark County residential sales have joined in a new real estate venture, taking more than a third of the space in downtown's Pacific Tower. In just three weeks, 30 agents have set up offices in the space. Mark McLoud, formerly of Prudential Northwest Properties, will serve as broker.

The Columbian
Jan. 20, 2005
Vancouver, Wash.

Chapter 8

The Importance of Being a Storyteller

Once Upon a Time ...

News organizations, which are a gateway between individuals and publicity, are storytellers who tell their stories to readers, viewers, and listeners. This chapter explains why real estate agents and brokers should be their own storyteller.

Every television station, radio station, magazine, or newspaper that you'd like to have do a story about you or your company has an important thing in common: each is a storyteller which seeks to find and report stories that will be of interest to their audiences.

That's why one of the most important keys to your success in generating publicity is your ability to tell your story. To be, in effect, a storyteller.

Can you tell stories about your real estate services, expertise, activities, or accomplishments in such a way that they attract the interest of news organizations? If you can, then you will likely be able to convince them to tell your story to your target audience.

Telling your own story to the media is truly a classic "win-win" opportunity for people who want publicity.

- By telling your real estate-related story to the storytellers, you are helping them do their job.

- And by telling your story to their audiences, those news organizations are helping to publicize you or establish or maintain the image or reputation you want for you or your company.

The Bottom Line

- News organizations are storytellers.
- You must be your own storyteller.
- To help generate the publicity you want, you must tell your story effectively to editors and journalists.

How to Generate Publicity: Celebrate an Anniversary or Other Milestone

50 Years Later: Conway In It For Work: His Independent Firm Has $2B Annual Sales
Fifty years ago this month, a 32-year-old ex-boxing reporter named Jack Conway
opened a Hingham storefront real estate office with one employee—himself. Five
decades later, Jack Conway & Co. has grown into the state's largest independent
real estate firm, with 45 offices and 960 workers who sell some $2 billion worth
of homes per year "We've been blessed," Conway said this past week as his
Norwell-based firm marked its 50th birthday.

Boston Herald
Oct. 15, 2006
Boston, Mass.

Advice and Insights: One of the toughest stories to get the media to cover can be
an anniversary or other milestone that is being celebrated by a corporation or
organization. That's because most reporters regard these as self-congratulatory
events that interest no one.

Sometimes, however, a well-written news release (see Chapter 34) about an
anniversary can convince a journalist to write a story about an important
anniversary or milestone that you or your company is observing. At other
times, you may need to stage a special event or provide an interesting visual to
get the attention of reporters.

Since entire books have been written about how to plan and stage special
events to mark these corporate milestones, I won't try to duplicate their advice
here. Suffice it to say, however, that the most effective way to grab the attention of
the media is to ensure that the events:

- Are staged so that it will be as easy as possible for news organizations to
  cover and photograph the festivities.
- Have good visuals, such as people standing in front of a new housing
  development.
- Have a local tie-in to the community, such as a fundraiser on behalf of a
  local affordable housing project.
- Are well organized.
- Are planned far enough in advance (as least four to six weeks before the
  event).

- Involve employees and customers in some way.
- Are consistent with the image, reputation, or history of the company or organization.

Chapter 9

The Importance of Research

Do You Have Any Idea What You're Talking About?

Credibility and expertise are two key ingredients in the efforts by real estate agents to generate publicity. This chapter talks about the importance of research to help bolster your claims, prove your points, and strengthen your arguments.

Home Price: Is $1,000,000 Next?
[Broker Patti] Cohn [of Frank Howard Allen's Greenbrae office] said that "what is uncommon about Marin is that people will wait to sell. They are not desperate." She cited Multiple Listing Service figures, noting that, last month, 47 percent of homes listed sold within 30 days at 1.2 percent over the asking price.

Marin Independent Journal
May 19, 2006
San Rafael, Calif.

Most reporters and columnists will not accept anything you tell them on face value. In fact, an editor once told me that he'd often warn his reporters: "If your mother says she loves you, check it out!"

When you tell your story to the media, you will face the same kind of skepticism. An effective way to show the media you know what you are talking about is to have the appropriate real estate background, credentials, or accurate and current facts and figures necessary to prove your points, make your arguments, or bolster your claims.

The research you'll need depends on the story you want to pitch to the media.

For instance, before you are interviewed by reporters about your take on trends on the local real estate market, you'd best consult your local Multiple Listing Service or your network of colleagues.

Don't be shy about using your research early and often in your news releases or other press materials, such as press kits and fact sheets. Why? Because the sooner you can convince reporters you know what you're talking about, the more likely it is that your news release will result in news coverage and journalists will contact you for interviews.

The credibility of your research is just as important as any of facts or figures you use.

For example, a newsletter issued by the Princeton Dental Resource Center reported the results of a study that found that chocolate might help fight cavities. Reporters at *The New York Times* discovered that the study had been financed by the Mars candy company, and the news-making cavity fighting claims quickly lost their credibility.

The Bottom Line

- You will need relevant facts, figures, and other research to help tell your story to the media and enhance your credibility.

- The research you need will depend on what you want to publicize.

How to Generate Publicity: Write a Book

How to Spot Red Flags on a Property
Anthony Marguleas, broker, Realtor and owner of Amalfi Estates in Los Angeles and author of a forthcoming book called "Secrets and Myths of Real Estate," said to walk around the area before making an offer and take note of how other homes in the neighborhood are maintained.

NBC-17
Nov. 2, 2006
Raleigh, N.C.

Advice and Insights: Writing a book can provide an effective news hook that may attract the interest of news outlets and Web sites in doing stories about you, while highlighting your real estate expertise and accomplishments at the same time.

Being a published author automatically confers upon real estate agents and brokers an instant credibility in the eyes of editors, reporters, and columnists. Many journalists assume that since you wrote a book, you are an expert on the topic and therefore must know what you are talking about. Reporters reason that if you know what you are talking about, you can probably provide important information, insights, and perspectives on that or related topics for their stories.

But it doesn't have to stop there.

- Depending on the topic and current events, authors are frequent guests on the radio talk show and television news and interview program circuit.

- By turning chapters of your book into stand-alone articles, you can often get extra mileage out of the work you did in writing the book, while receiving additional attention from the media.

- At listing presentations, you can impress potential clients by giving them a copy of your book (it sure beats a PowerPoint presentation or marketing brochure).

Some agents, instead of writing their own books, may be featured in someone else's book on real estate. Contributing to or being interviewed for that book can be legitimate reasons for issuing a news release and seeking publicity. For example:

Jane Fairweather Recognized as Billion Dollar Agent in Real Estate Industry
Bethesda, MD—Jane Fairweather, a top Realtor in Bethesda, Maryland, is recognized and interviewed in the forthcoming book, *Billion Dollar Agent—Lessons Learned.* Jane Fairweather has been a Realtor for 25 years and has career sales of about $1.2 billion and over 2,500 homes sold. Jane operates her company The

Jane Fairweather Team as part of the Coldwell Banker Residential Brokerage Franchise. Her website, http://www.janefairweather.com provides detailed information about buying and selling tips for the area.

In the book, Jane reflects on her own experience and lessons learned. "I learned how to run a business by being self-employed in my previous career. When I began my real estate career I had no money but a lot of time. So, I did direct mail and handwrote and stamped the cards myself. Direct mail put me on the top of peoples' minds with regard to real estate," said Jane.

PRWeb
Nov. 2, 2006

Chapter 10

Why You Should Prioritize Your Information

Keep it Simple, Stupid

This chapter shows how real estate professionals can ensure that stories are reported the way they want by limiting, summarizing, and prioritizing the information they provide to news organizations.

When you tell your story to editors, reporters, or columnists, it is important to guard against the tendency to tell them *everything* about your story.

For example, if you tell a newspaper reporter 15 different reasons why your real estate services are different or better than your competition, you'll have no idea which one of those 15 reasons he'll decide to use in his story. That's because the reporter must confine his story to the length assigned by his editor. To do that, of course, he must decide what information you tell him will be most important to pass along to his readers.

However, if you don't tell the reporter what *you* think are the most important points, then you are leaving the decision about what's important up to him, and you'll have *no idea* which of the information you gave him will wind up in an article. When the story comes out, you could be upset that the reporter did not include what you thought was most important.

Ric Edelman, a national television talk show host and author of *Ordinary People, Extraordinary Wealth,* says it's also important that you feel strongly about what you tell the media—and that it shows. Edelman notes, "If you don't believe in what you are saying and don't have a passion for it, then you are not going to accomplish very much. You must be willing to give it the amount of effort that it needs, and to sustain those efforts for as long as necessary. Otherwise, people will see that you don't have the passion and won't believe in your message."

To make sure that your story comes out the way you want:

1. Prioritize the information you'd like the reporter to include in the story.

2. Limit the information you tell the reporter to no more than three major points. This will help ensure that the points that are most important to you are the ones that the reporter will most likely include in the article.

3. Keep reinforcing those points to the reporter when he calls with questions or interviews you for his story.

Former TV news reporter Karen Friedman offers this advice: "Some people give reporters too much information. Sometimes during an interview, a person might rattle off eight or nine talking points. They left it up to me to decide which point was most important. If I picked point number eight, inevitably that person would call me to complain that I missed his point.

"In reality, he missed his point because if he had focused on one clear message, I would have easily delivered that message for him."

The Bottom Line

- If you give too much information to journalists, you will have no idea what they will use in their stories.

- Prioritize and limit the information you give to reporters to three major points.

How to Generate Publicity: Sponsor an Essay Contest

Lakewood Ranch Grad Wins Contest

Lakewood Ranch High School graduate Joshua Rosenauer was one of four state winners in the Florida Association of Realtors' essay contest and scholarship program. The winners received $5,000 scholarships based on their essays about how Realtors benefit the community. Rosenauer's essay focused on how his neighbors who are Realtors help make the community feel like a home and how they've taken an active role in the community.

The Herald
Oct. 15, 2006
Bradenton, Fla.

Advice and Insights: There are many ways for real estate companies and associations to help promote themselves and the issues that are important to REALTORS®. One way is to sponsor student essay contests and announce the winners in news releases that are sent to local news outlets. The larger the scholarships or cash prizes, the more news value your contest will likely have.

Chapter 11

How to Get the Media's Attention

News Hooks and Story Angles

This chapter discusses the best ways to convince journalists to do stories about you or your company, and includes a list of more than two dozen proven story hooks and news angles.

Attracting the attention of editors or reporters is like trying to catch fish. There are any number of different hooks, lures, and bait you can use to get the job done.

One of the best ways to convince journalists to do stories about you is to use a story angle or news hook or launch an activity or project that reflects your expertise, activities, or accomplishments.

I've reviewed thousands of stories that have been done over the last few years about real estate companies, agents and brokers. I found that the news hooks, story angles, activities, and projects that resulted in news coverage about them fall into one of the following major categories:

1. Share your real estate expertise.

2. Discuss trends and developments.

3. Start a new service.

4. Announce the hiring of new agents.

5. Advocate affordable housing.

6. Promote your professional designations.

7. Start a new real estate company.

8. Open a new office.

9. Celebrate an anniversary or other milestone.

10. Sponsor events projects and activities.

11. Make a speech.

12. Write a book.

13. Conduct a study or survey.

14. Build homes for the needy.

15. Raise money for a good cause.

16. Market yourself or your listings in unique ways or unusual places.

17. Use technology to market yourself or your listings.

18. Showcase unusual properties.

19. Provide insights and perspectives on housing-related topics.

20. Promote performance and sales figures.

21. Ride on another's coattails.

22. Make predictions or forecasts.

23. Issue a call to action.

24. Conduct seminars and workshops.

25. Move your office.

26. Merge with other companies.

27. Form joint ventures and alliances.

28. Have interesting hobbies and sidelines.

29. Sponsor essay contests.

30. Help clean up the neighborhood.

31. Comment on recent real estate transactions.

Examples of these categories, including the headlines and brief excerpts from newspaper stories that have been published about real estate agents and brokers, are featured throughout the book in sections called *How to Generate Publicity*. For example:

How to Generate Publicity: Raise Money for a Good Cause

Real Estate Agents To Put On Benefit For Hospice

More than 150 Marin real estate professionals are volunteering for a three-day benefit this weekend expected to raise more than $100,000 for Hospice of Marin in Larkspur. The "Open Hearts, Open Homes" fundraiser features Eichler home tours Saturday in celebration of the 50th anniversary of the distinctive homes built by Joseph Eichler.

"The public has always had an interest in Eichlers because of their unusual architecture and because people who live in them do really interesting things with their Eichler homes," said Catherine Munson, honorary chairwoman of the event and owner of Lucas Valley Properties. "A group of people in the real estate industry came up with the idea to honor Eichler homes on their 50th birthday and to have an event with broad appeal so we could make the money we were trying to make for the Hospice of Marin."

The Marin Independent Journal
Sept. 14, 2006
San Rafael, Calif.

Review these news clips for important insights into the types of stories news organizations have done about other agents, brokers, and REALTOR® associations in different parts of the country.

As you read through the examples:

- See which ones may be a good fit for you or your real estate company.

- Start thinking about how you can adapt and customize them for your real estate business to help generate publicity about your expertise, services, opinion, activities, or accomplishments.

- If you are already implementing the projects or activities that are the basis for the news hooks, then take steps to get the word out to the media about what you are doing. (See Chapter 34)

- If you find out that a reporter is working on a topic-related story, ask to be interviewed for the story and craft your remarks as necessary.

- If you want to emulate the activities other real estate professionals have used to capture the attention of news organizations, take steps to organize or implement similar projects.

- Identify or create visuals that help you to show your story. (See Chapter 12)
- Then use the advice in other parts of this book to help tell your story in an effective and attention-getting way.

The Bottom Line

- A good story is the bait you need to help attract the interest of news organizations in doing a story about you or your real estate company.
- There are dozens of effective story angles and news hooks that real estate professionals have used to help generate publicity about themselves.
- Look for *How to Generate Publicity* sections throughout the book for news hooks you can customize and use for yourself.

How to Generate Publicity: Comment on Recent Real Estate Transactions

Kozlowski Sells Colorado Home For $10 million
L. Dennis Kozlowski, the imprisoned former chief executive officer of Tyco International Ltd. and a former Cumberland resident, is selling his Colorado mountain mansion for $10 million to raise money for fines and restitution. "At ten million, it's a decent house, although some people I talked to thought it wasn't worth more than eight," said David Nilges, a Colorado real estate broker not involved in the sale who toured the residence in January. "The view is to die for."

Bloomberg News
Nov. 8, 2006

Advice and Insights: Presenting yourself to the media as an expert on real estate-related topics is a time-tested way to help generate news coverage about yourself or your company.

Why? Because editors, reporters, and columnists are always looking for experts to interview and quote in their stories about real estate prices or inventories, and a wide range of related trends, developments, news, forecasts, warnings, or predictions. While there may not be any $10 million homes in your community, there may very well be a property for sale, or one that has just been sold, that may be worth a story. If you know about such a property, call the local real estate reporter and suggest they do a story about it—and that they interview you for the article.

Your sound bites or ink bites can help enliven their reports, add perspective or color to their articles, and provide important insights and information to their audiences.

But in order for you to be interviewed about your expertise by reporters for their stories, you have to do four things:

1. Know what you are talking about and legitimately position yourself as an expert on a real estate-related topic.

2. Know how to talk in sound bites or ink bites (see Chapter 22).

3. Let reporters know you exist and are available for interviews.

4. Return reporters' calls or e-mail messages immediately.

Assuming you are an expert and have mastered the art of sound bites, your biggest challenge may be to let reporters and columnists know who you are and how to reach you (see Chapter 25).

Chapter 12

Why You Need Visuals

Picture This!

Unless you can show your story, you will only communicate half your story to the media and target audience. This chapter explains why pictures are important to television, newspapers, and even radio, and how effective visuals can help attract the attention of editors and reporters.

Good storytellers know not only how to *tell* their story, but also how to *show* it.

And the fact of the matter is that unless you can show your story, you will only communicate half your story to the media and your target audience. Why?

- Since television is obviously a visual medium, your ability to find pictures to help tell your story will make it easier for TV reporters to decide to do a story about you.

- The same holds true for newspapers, where a picture that shows some aspect of your story will make any article they do about you that much longer and eye-catching to the reader.

- And since radio reporters are in the business of painting word pictures for their listeners, your ability to provide a visual image that illustrates your story will make the reporter's job easier as well.

In addition to helping attract the attention of the media to your story, sending an appropriate photo and descriptive caption (also known as a cut line) can also result in a larger story to accommodate the picture, and encourage more people to read the story in the first place, since people are often attracted by pictures and graphics.

Before going to the expense of taking and sending a photo, however, it's wise to check with the publication to make sure they are interested in receiving it and whether they prefer color or black-and-white photos, slides, transparencies, or a digital version on computer disk or via e-mail.

For the latest examples of photos and cut lines, click on the "tools of the trade" link on the home page of www.ProfitByPublicity.com. Also, be sure to visit my blog at http://ProfitByPublicity.blogspot.com.

Exercise: Visualizing Visuals

List all of the possible visuals you can think of that will help show your story. Then prioritize the ones that will be most important or effective in helping to publicize yourself, your services, accomplishments, activities, expertise, or company

For example:

Story	Visual
Hiring a new agent	Head and shoulder photo
Fundraising project for local charity	Presentation of oversized check to officials
Agents donate time to help build Habitat for Humanity home	Agents working on home
Advice on staging a home	Before/after photos
Broker sponsors Toys for Tots campaign	Agents collecting toys
Record quarterly sales	Chart showing increased sales
Company donates backpacks to school	Employees preparing back packs

The Bottom Line

- Good visuals will help you tell your story to the media more efficiently and effectively.

- Identify or create the pictures or other visuals that are most appropriate for what you want to publicize.

- Pictures and other visuals can help you get longer and better stories in newspapers.

How to Generate Publicity: Conduct a Study or Survey

Senior Real Estate Attitudes Changing
Attitudes about real estate and the home-buying and selling process are changing among people 50 years of age and older, according to a survey released by ERA Real Estate.

Inman News
Feb. 10, 2005

Advice and Insights: Every year newspapers, magazines, newsletters, and TV and radio stations report the results of the newest study or research project that has just been released by a company or organization on variety of topics.

Reporters and columnists will often include in their stories the comments and observations of the organization's officials about the significance, impact, or meaning of the report's findings, conclusions, recommendations, or call for action.

The results of a newsworthy poll can provide a quick, easy, and legitimate news hook for reporters and columnists who usually will give proper credit to a REALTOR®, a real estate broker, or real estate company who commissioned the study in the first place. Often, the journalists will call the broker or company official to interview them about the results and include their comments in the story.

In addition to helping generate news coverage about your company, an opinion poll can be an excellent way to gather information you need to support or substantiate your credibility on an issue (see Chapter 9) and gain valuable insights into what the public thinks on a given topic.

Before you commission a poll, however, make sure that:

- The results are likely to be newsworthy.
- The topic is relevant to your own areas of expertise.

There are several professional polling organizations—including online survey services—that can prepare and conduct an opinion poll for you or your real estate company.

Chapter 13

Prepare Your Publicity Plan

Plot Your Course

Explains why you need a written plan to generate publicity and includes a worksheet to help prepare it.

If you were planning to drive from one part of the country to another, like most people you would take some time to prepare for the trip. Your checklist might include mapping out a route, making sure your car was in good working order, arranging for someone to look out for your house while you were away, packing the clothes you'd need, etc.

A similar list will come in just as handy as you prepare to generate news coverage about yourself or your company. Take a few minutes now to familiarize yourself with the following checklist and, as you read through this handbook, go back and fill in each item. The result will help you prepare your own personal plan for generating the publicity you want. (Sample answers are in italics.)

- Why do you want to generate news coverage about yourself or your company?
  To help generate more clients.

- How do you want to use that news coverage?
  In my listing presentation to help impress potential clients.

- What aspect of your personal or professional life do you want that news coverage to focus on?
  I want to stress my professionalism and the real estate training and education I've received.

- How will you know when you've generated your desired level of publicity?
  When people start calling me to ask that I list their property.

- What are the three most important things you want to communicate to your target audience?
  The importance of the REALTOR® Code of Ethics, the professional designations I've earned, and how I am different and better than my competition.
- What is your brand identity? *I am a Senior Real Estate Specialist.*
- How much publicity do you want? *I want to be quoted on a regular basis in the local daily newspaper.*
- Who is your target audience? *First-time home buyers, especially Generation X'ers.*
- Where do they live? *Throughout the county.*
- Which news organizations do they read, watch, or listen to? *The local daily newspaper, radio stations, and various Web sites.*
- What facts and figures will you need to *tell* your story? *Statistics about the benefits and advantages of home ownership, and why now is a good time to buy.*
- What visuals can you use to help *show* your story? *Charts and graphs and the latest opinion polls about home ownership.*
- What news hooks or story angles will you use to help attract the attention of the media? *Monthly statistics issued by my MLS, the National Association of REALTORS®, and reports from various federal agencies.*
- What sound bites will you use during interviews? *Because of continued falling prices, this is the best time to buy a home in the last ten years.*
- Who is your competition? *The 500 other real estate agents in my area.*
- How is your story different or better than theirs? *Most of them are so worried about how declining prices impact sellers, and are not focusing in on the impact on buyers.*
- What tactics will you use to communicate your messages? *I will become a resource to reporters who cover real estate in my area and issue news releases on a quarterly basis about my observations of the local housing market and their impact on buyers. I will also try to write and place one op-ed a year in the daily newspaper about real estate trends and developments.*

How much time will you need to research, draft, prepare, or implement these tactics? Following are estimated lead times for the most frequently used tactics, and where you can learn more about them in this book:

Tactic	Lead Time
• News releases (Chapter 34)	1 to 3 days
• Fact sheets (Chapter 35)	3 to 5 days
• Press kits (Chapter 36)	1 to 3 days
• News advisories (Chapter 37)	1 to 2 days
• Biographical profiles (Chapter 38)	5 to 7 days
• Op-eds and bylined articles (Chapter 39)	7 to 10 days
• Letters to the editor (Chapter 40)	1 to 2 days
• Video news releases (Chapter 41)	7 to 21 days
• Audio news releases (Chapter 41)	2 to 4 days
• News conferences (Chapter 42)	1 to 7 days
• Satellite media tours (Chapter 43)	1 to 7 days
• Story pitch calls and letters (Chapter 45)	1 to 2 days
• Newsletters and Web sites (Chapter 47)	7 to 14 days
• Research editorial calendars (Chapter 48)	1 to 7 days
• Become a resource to the media (Chapter 25)	1 to 7 days
• Deliver speeches to local groups (Chapter 17)	30 to 120 days

- What research information will you need? (Chapter 9)
  I may have to hire a freelance writer to help prepare the op-eds I'd like to place.

- How much will you need to spend? (See Chapter 4)
  About $2,500 a year.

- What approvals, if any, do you need to obtain within your company before you can implement this plan? What is the approval process and how much time will it take?
  My broker wants me to keep her posted about my publicity activities, but does not need to approve my press releases or op-eds.

- If you won't implement this plan yourself, which PR consultant or agency will you work with? (See Chapter 15)
  I will contact the nearest chapter of the Public Relations Society of America to find a qualified freelance writer to help me with my press releases and op-eds.

Schedule of Activities

Based on what you want to do and how long it may take you to do it, insert reasonable deadlines for each project or activity in the following sample schedule of activities.

Activity	Deadline
News release	
Draft	
Distribute	
Fact Sheet	
Draft	
Distribute	
Post on Web site	
Press Kit	
Draft	
Distribute	
Post on Web site	
Op-ed/bylines article	
Draft	
Send to editor	
Letters to the editor	
Draft	
Send to editor	
Make story pitch calls	
Prepare list of reporters to contact	
Call or send e-mails to list	
Join local organizations	
Select list of organizations to join	
Contact for membership information	
Fill out and return membership applications	
Schedule speeches to local groups	
Select groups to speak to	
Contact group re speaking opportunities	
Schedule speech	
Blog	
Set up blog on Web site	
Prepare list of topics to write about	
Create and post content on the blog	

The Bottom Line

- You need a plan to ensure that you generate the publicity that you want.
- Make allowances in your plan for how much time various activities are likely to take.

How to Generate Publicity: Build Homes for the Needy

Realtors Build House for Katrina Victims
Other days they sell homes, but on Oct. 24 Realtors from the Pocono Mountains Association of Realtors joined forces to build a House in a Box with Habitat for Humanity. The nails connected more than walls. They linked Realtors from northeastern Pennsylvania with a family in Louisiana whose home was destroyed by flooding after Hurricane Katrina.

"The most memorable part of the day was seeing Realtors autographing the two-by-fours," said Broker Thomas R. Wilkins, president of Wilkins & Associates Real Estate, the largest real estate company in northeastern Pennsylvania, which sent 15 volunteers to the build.

Pocono Record
Nov. 4, 2006
Stroudsburg, Pa.

Advice and Insights: Although many news organizations are often criticized for reporting negative news, these same news outlets also do stories about groups, organizations, and companies that are working to help improve their communities.

Ironically, real estate agents and brokers across the country frequently donate their time, money, or efforts on behalf of a variety of important community projects, but fail to let the media know about these efforts.

Telling the media about what you are doing to help others in the community can be an effective way to generate publicity about yourself or your company.

Chapter 14

Test-Market Your Plan

Better Safe than Sorry

This chapter shows how by test-marketing their plan, real estate agents can help ensure it will work; explains why testing will help make the plan stronger and more effective.

Okay, you've filled in all the blanks, answered all the questions, and are ready to implement your PR plan.

But before you do, it's time to ask yourself some important questions.

Are you sure that you've answered, to the best of your ability, the questions of who cares and why? (See Chapter 3)

Are you confident that your news hook is the most effective it can be? (See Chapter 11)

Are you positive that your news release will make the media sit up and take notice? (See Chapter 34)

There are two ways to find out for sure.

The first is to simply execute your plan full blast, at warp speed, as soon as possible. Send out those faxes! Distribute those e-mails! Fill the mailboxes with your news releases!

But how will you feel if those releases come back as being undeliverable because of wrong addresses? How will you react if reporters ignore your story? What if your quotes wind up on the cutting room floor?

The *best* way to help guarantee your success is to do what many Fortune 500 companies do before they launch a multimillion dollar marketing campaign.

They'll try it on a small scale before unleashing it on the rest of the world.

It's called test-marketing.

1. Instead of sending out hundreds of news releases, send out a handful to see how they are received. Follow-up on the releases with phone calls to the

people who received them and ask if they are interested in doing a story. If not, why not?

2. Put yourself in the shoes of the reporter who will receive your news release. If you were the reporter, what questions would you ask?

3. Arrange for your friends or colleagues to play reporter with you to see how well you are able to answer their questions.

4. Are you sending releases to the people who will be most interested in receiving them?

5. Don't trust whatever sources you used to compile your media list and assume you have the most current or accurate contact information. Call each reporter on the list and make sure that he or she is the best person at that news organization to receive the information you will send.

6. Try to arrange at least one interview with a reporter to see how well your news release or sound bites are received.

7. Are the visuals you selected to show your story hitting a responsive cord? If not, why not?

You get the idea.

Why roll the dice when you could stack the deck and help ensure your success? By taking a little time now to test-market your plan, you can then take whatever steps may be necessary to make it as strong and effective today so that you won't be surprised or disappointed tomorrow.

The Bottom Line

- Test-market your publicity plan before you implement it.
- Learn from the successes and failures of your test, and modify your plan as necessary.

How to Generate Publicity: Help Clean Up Your Community

GLOUCESTER TOWNSHIP—The church committee that's been cleaning up the old township building on Church Street received some extra help last Thursday. About 30 members of the Prudential, Fox & Roach REALTORS Gloucester Township office removed their business suits and dresses in exchange for torn-up jeans and old T-shirts. The group cleaned-up the first floor of the entire right-side of the building.

Record Breeze
Oct. 12, 2006
Camden, N.J.

Advice and Insights: You don't need to spend money in order to have an impact on your community. Sometimes all that is needed are brooms, a little elbow grease, and a commitment to clear your calendar. It's a good bet that there are any number of groups and organizations in your town or city who would welcome your helping hands with open arms. The more people in your office or company that you can get involved in a clean-up project, the more newsworthy your help will be to local news organizations.

Chapter 15

How to Find and Work with PR Agencies and Consultants

If You're Too Busy to Do It Yourself…

> If real estate agents don't have the time, talent or energy to generate publicity on their own, they can use a PR agency or consultant.

If you don't have the time, resources, or patience to generate publicity about yourself, there are thousands of public relations agencies and consultants who can try to do the job for you. However, hiring a consultant does not mean you should stop reading this book.
By finishing the book you will:

- Be better equipped to work with a PR firm, since you will have a better understanding of what's involved in generating publicity.

- Gain insights into the story angles or news hooks that are more likely to result in news coverage.

- Know how to prepare for media interviews that your PR firm may be able to arrange.

It is relatively easy to find a number of agencies or individuals to talk to and interview for the job. (See the resources section at the end of this chapter.)

Depending on the amount and frequency of news coverage you want and the caliber of the consultant or agency you want to hire, the fee for their services can range anywhere from less than $100 an hour to more than $10,000 a month.

It's one thing to find agencies with which to talk. It's quite another to select the best one for your needs. Following is a suggested checklist of questions and issues you should consider as you look for the best agency or consultant to represent you.

- What kind of results have they achieved for other clients? Ask to see relevant case studies.
- How long has the company been in business?
- What awards or recognition have they received for their work?
- How much turnover do they have in their list of current clients? How long has the agency or consultant worked for their oldest client?
- How many editors, reporters, and columnists do they know? (This is a trick question, since the number of reporters an agency knows usually has nothing to do with their ability to generate results for you. It is much more important that they know how to find the right reporter who will be interested in your story, and that they know how to pitch your story in such a way as to get the interest of the media.)
- What do they consider to be their strengths and weaknesses?
- Have they worked for other real estate-related clients? (This is another trick question. A good PR person should be like a good reporter: with the right facts and information, he or she should be able to create stories for clients no matter what line of business they're in.)
- Will the people who market their services to you be the same people who will work on your account?
- What is the background of the individuals who would work on your account on a day-to-day basis? What are their qualifications?
- Do they charge for their services on an hourly, project, or retainer basis?
- Do they want a performance bonus as an incentive to meet or exceed your expectations?
- What is their level of understanding of your own business or the real estate profession (the more they know about you and your business, the more likely it is they can recommend story ideas and news hooks to publicize you).
- Ask to see writing samples from the people who will be working on your account.
- Do they seem to be over-promising results?
- Get everything in writing.
- Is there a 30-day cancellation clause in the contract to terminate the relationship with the agency or consultant?
- Is there good chemistry between you and the people who will work on the account?

- How many turnovers are there among the agency's staff?
- How often will they report to you about their activities and results?
- Do they work for other clients who would pose a conflict if they worked for you?
- Given the work they do for other clients, will they have time to give your account the time, attention and resources it deserves?
- Ask to see a sample of their invoices. Are they clear and easy to understand?
- How creative and flexible are they in coming up with new and different ways to achieve results for clients or in adapting to changing situations? Ask for recent examples.
- Ask for references. And call them.

After you've asked your questions of the agency, be prepared to answer some questions they may have for you, including:

- Background information about you or your company.
- Your goals and objectives.
- Your expectations and timeframe for results.
- How much you are prepared to spend in fees and expenses.

Once you've hired a PR firm, you, or your new consultant, may want to generate publicity about the arrangement:

Barb Bashor Hires CTA Public Relations for Luxury Homes Marketing Brand Development and Awareness Campaign
Louisville, CO—CTA Public Relations has been retained by realtor Barb Bashor to design and develop a corporate branding strategy and awareness campaign for her luxury home marketing division. CTA will design and develop a company logo, marketing brochure, web site and additional collateral materials that reflect the real estate company's new initiative in the exclusive luxury home market, focusing on properties valued above $1,000,000.

PR Newswire
Aug. 14, 2006
Denver, Colo.

Resources

In seeking the services of a public relations expert or agency, consider contacting the following organizations or individuals:

- Public Relations Society of America (www.prsa.org).
- International Association of Business Communicators (www.iabc.com).
- O'Dwyer's Directory of Public Relations Agencies (www.odwyerpr.com).
- Friends or colleagues who have used PR agencies or consultants.
- Your local or state chambers of commerce or Better Business Bureau.

The Bottom Line

- You may have to hire a PR firm or consultant if you don't have the time, skill or resources to generate publicity by yourself for you or your real estate firm.
- There are various sources you can consult to find candidates.
- To help decide who to hire, interview several firms about their qualifications, credentials, fees, etc.

How to Generate Publicity: Market Your Listings in Unique Ways

To Sell a High-end Home, Let Them Sleep on It
It took a sleepover to sell a $2.5 million house in Malibu, Calif., after it had been on the market for three months. The buyers "were able to experience the amazing light at different times of the day, the spectacular views and what it was like to really live there," said Frank Langen, the real estate agent who closed the deal and a partner at Deasy Penner and Partners, a boutique real estate firm in Los Angeles.

The New York Times
Dec. 29, 2005
New York, New York

Advice and Insights: Whether out of inspiration or desperation, real estate agents and brokers will often come up with interesting or unusual ways to promote their properties or close a deal.

While these creative approaches can provide real estate professionals with a competitive edge, their marketing tactics can be the basis of news hooks that can attract the attention of editors and reporters.

Sometimes your use of technology to market a listing will provide the story angle reporters need to write a story about you. For example:

DVDs Becoming Major Marketing Tool For Real Estate
Michael Garden, an agent with Prudential Fox & Roach, saw DVDs being used to advertise big real estate projects, and he saw no reason why he shouldn't give them a try, too. "When a buyer has so many choices in a specific price range, in reasonably close proximity, the DVD might be the thing that helps them remember what they saw that day," Garden said. The same is true for a buyer's agent, who each week has an extremely long list of new properties to preview, he said.

DVDs such as Garden's are just one way real estate agents are turning technology into a sales tool for a residential market in which listings are piling up. E-mail, Web sites, cell phones, high-speed wireless connections, and virtual tours are offering unprecedented ways to market and sell houses.

Philadelphia Inquirer
Oct. 22, 2006
Philadelphia, Pa.

Part II

Get Your Act Together before You Take It on the Road

What Your Mother Never Told You about Publicity

Chapter 16

Know Your Audience

It May be English to You, But It's All Greek to Them

Many people assume that anyone who speaks English should automatically understand the references, allusions, or comparisons they make to popular culture or history. Find out why this is not always the case.

As important as it is to know what you are talking about (see Chapter 9), it's just as critical that your target audience can *understand* what you're talking about.

Every industry and profession—including real estate—has a list of acronyms and buzzwords that people in those industries often use when talking to each other.

But if you use real estate jargon and acronyms in a speech, news release, or other communications with the general public, the chances are pretty good that they will have no idea what you are talking about. Why make it any harder to get your message across than necessary?

For example, the Web site of the California Association of REALTORS® lists and defines real estate words and phrases that are likely to draw a blank stare from the average person. The list includes:

CCR	Conditions, Covenants, and Restrictions
CAVE (people)	Californians Against Virtually Everything
CLTA	California Land Title Association
BANANA	Build Absolutely Nothing Anywhere Near Anybody
FMV	Fair Market Value
HOA	Home Owners Association
NAR	National Association of REALTORS®
RESPA	Real Estate Settlement Procedures Act
VRM	Variable Rate Mortgage

Even when you speak in plain and simple English, some members of your target audience may not be able to understand what you are talking about if you refer to places, people, things, or events for which they have no frame of reference.

To help ensure their faculty members are in sync with the cultural touchstones of students, each year Beloit College in Beloit, Wisconsin issues a list of items about which students born in a particular year may not be aware.

For example, students born in 1980 (some of whom may be or about to be your clients):

- Have no meaningful recollection of the Reagan era, and did not know he had ever been shot.
- Were 11 when the Soviet Union broke apart, and do not remember the Cold War.
- Have never feared a nuclear war. "The Day After" is a pill to them—not a movie.
- Are too young to remember the space shuttle *Challenger* blowing up.
- Have always known of AIDS.
- Never had a polio shot and do not know what it is.
- Always used plastic bottle caps.
- Does not know what the expression "you sound like a broken record" means.
- Have never owned a record player.
- Likely never played Pac Man, and have never heard of "Pong."
- Think Star Wars looks very fake, and the special effects are pathetic.
- Have always known about VCRs, but they have no idea what Beta is.
- Cannot fathom what it was like not having a remote control.
- Were born the year the Walkman was introduced by Sony.
- The Vietnam War is as ancient history to them as WWI and WWII or even the Civil War.
- Never heard the terms "Where's the Beef?," "I'd walk a mile for a a Camel" or "De plane, boss! De plane!"
- Do not care who shot J.R. and have no idea who J.R. was.
- Think of Kansas, Boston, Chicago, America, and Alabama as places—not music groups.
- Never had a McDonald's meal in a Styrofoam® container.

What do you know about the frames of reference of your target audiences, and how can you use that knowledge to ensure that your story is both heard and understood?

The Bottom Line

- Make it as easy as possible for people to know what you are talking about by avoiding jargon and acronyms in your speeches or press materials.

- By knowing your audience, you will have a good idea about the most appropriate cultural and other references you can use when you communicate with them.

How to Generate Publicity: Showcase Unusual Properties

Grateful Dead Offices to Be Sold
The vintage San Rafael building where members of the Grateful Dead rented offices for more than 30 years is on the market for $1.15 million. "It's one of the great old properties of San Rafael," said listing agent Matt Storms of Keegan & Coppin Co., Inc. in Larkspur. How often do you run across a deal where the property owners for more than the last 100 years have been the same family?"

Marin Independent Journal
April 14, 2004
San Rafael, Calif.

Advice and Insights: Your best news hook for generating publicity about yourself or your company could be one of your own listings. An interesting aspect of the property—such as its location, history, previous owners, architecture, landscaping, décor, etc.—can provide the information you need to suggest that a journalist do a story about the house.

Sometimes it's the listing price that can attract a reporter's interest and result in publicity for the listing agent, as happened with this property New England:

For $25 Million, You Can Make This House Your Home
What does $25 million get you in Massachusetts? Nothing quite as exclusive as it would in the Virgin Islands, where for a million dollars less you can buy a private, 230-acre island. Still, the East Orleans property is nothing to sneer at. It's not just a home, it's a "retreat," according to the literature prepared by Century 21 Beach Road Real Estate/Fine Homes & Estates in Orleans, which is offering the estate jointly with [the seller's] California realtor, Kay Cole of Ewing & Associates/Sotheby's International Realty. Needless to say, homes of this caliber aren't sold the usual way. No "For Sale" signs or open houses, says Myra Brink-Dennis of Century 21.

The Globe
Nov. 11, 2006
New London, Conn.

Often it's the size of the property that will garner media attention. For example:

Got $2 Million? Town Could Be Yours
In the market for your own little slice of heaven? How about a whole town? The historic hub of Cazadero, a former sawmill town tucked in the redwoods of west Sonoma County, hit the auction block this week with an asking price of $2 million. Santa Rosa real estate agent Martin A. Levy say's he's received several calls already, mostly from people interested in opening a bed-and-breakfast or starting a restaurant.

The Press Democrat
Jan. 25, 2005
Santa Rosa, Calif.

Chapter 17

Overcome Your Fear of Speaking in Public

Speechless in Seattle (or Anywhere Else)

What should you do if you come down with a severe case of stage fright when asked to give a speech? Arnold Sanow, who overcame his fear of speaking in public to become a professional speaker, shares his secrets for success. This includes a checklist of items to keep in mind to help ensure you deliver successful presentations.

When asked to speak before large audiences, Arnold Sanow always seemed to come up with an excuse why he couldn't do it: he was too busy, not feeling well, had a conflicting engagement, was going out of town, or was not adequately prepared to make the presentation.

One day his luck ran out. At a company-wide staff meeting, Sanow was unexpectedly called on to speak about a project he was working on. By the time he arrived at the podium his mouth was dry, he was sweating profusely and his stomach felt like it was full of butterflies. When he opened his mouth to speak, the only sound he could hear was that of his heart, pounding in fear. "This," he reminded himself, "is why I hate to speak in public."

Opportunities to speak in public—from informal breakfast meetings to major keynote addresses—can be golden opportunities for you to let more people know about your real estate expertise, accomplishments, activities, or opinions.

Depending on the audience and topic, it is possible that reporters or editors from the local, business, and trade press will be in attendance, or that the event's organizers will send out a news release about your remarks. Indeed, you may want to work with the organizers to prepare and distribute your own news release to publicize your appearance, or send out a follow-up release summarizing your speech.

Why? Because news coverage about your speech can help ensure what you have to say will be communicated to a much larger audience than the one in the room.

But what happens if you get butterflies in your stomach—or worse—every time you are asked to speak in public?

Walter Cronkite, former anchor of CBS Evening News and a frequent public speaker once said, "It's natural to have butterflies. The secret is to get them to fly in formation."

Sanow, a professional speaker who conducts marketing workshops across the country, trained his own butterflies to fly in formation, and his experience can help you conquer your own fears of speaking in public.

For most of his life, Sanow suffered from acute anxiety whenever he had to speak in public. "I was afraid I would look like a fool, did not want to risk being rejected by my peers, and always found excuses not to speak before large groups of people," he says.

But Sanow was determined not to let the butterflies ruin his life. To overcome his fears, he carefully followed a master checklist to help himself prepare, plan, and deliver presentations. The checklist includes the following items:

Prepare for Success

Rid yourself of beliefs that cause fear, such as:

- "I failed before when I spoke in public, so I will probably fail again."
- "A survey says that public speaking is the number one fear of most people, so it must be my number one fear."
- "The audience wants me to fail. The audience is my enemy."
- "I may make a mistake. I want to be perfect."

Instead:

- Replace negative thoughts with positive ones, such as "I am a great speaker."
- Practice speaking at every opportunity you can find before groups of people on a variety of topics and in different situations and circumstances.
- Meditate. Before each speech, use a relaxation exercise to tense up different parts of your body and then relax them.

Arnold Sanow's checklist worked, and he dramatically lowered the anxiety he felt whenever he got up to talk.

Not only did he get his butterflies to fly in formation, he went on to become a successful full-time professional speaker and president of the Business Source in Vienna, Va. Sanow delivers more than 150 paid presentations a year to corporations, organizations, and conferences and is one of only 300 people in the world to be designated a Certified Speaking Professional by the National Speakers Association.

But Sanow is not one to let go of a good thing. He says he still uses his fear-reducing techniques for every presentation he gives.

You never know when your butterflies might try to break formation.

To complement Sanow's advice, following is my own checklist of items to keep in mind before you accept any speaking invitation, and suggestions on how to prepare for and get the most out of your presentation.

Invitations

- Don't accept speaking invitations for which you are unqualified or unprepared (don't let your ego get in the way).
- Think twice about giving breakfast speeches if you are not a morning person, or evening presentations if you like to retire early.
- Ask the organizers if there is anything special you should know about the audience or the group (forewarned is forearmed).
- Ask others who have spoken to the organization what it was like, and what you can learn from their experience.
- If you accept the invitation, know what you want to accomplish by giving the presentation.
- Know the basics of the speaking situation (format, length, time, location, etc.).
- Ask for directions to the event, use Mapquest, etc.

Audience

- Know the audience (find out as much as you can about their demographics, interests, experiences, knowledge of the topic you will be talking about, etc.).
- Find out how many people are expected to be in the audience.

Emergency

- Exchange cell phone numbers with the host/organizer (in case of emergencies, last minute changes or questions, etc.).

Publicity

- Make the most of your presentation before and after you give it, including news releases, e-mail and newsletter announcements, Web site postings, press interviews, etc. (all PR about your presentation is good PR).

Location

- Make sure that the layout of the room is to your liking (classroom-style, theatre-style, round tables, etc.).
- Always show up early (arrive early to walk the room, meet people, etc).
- Do show up at the right place at the right time (allow for traffic, road construction, weather, etc.).
- When you arrive, check with your host to ensure that the arrangements and purpose of your presentation have not changed (no sudden surprises).
- Check out any stairs you must climb to get on or off the stage (help prevent tripping over unfamiliar steps).
- Know where things are (lights, mike, AC, heating, restrooms).
- Guarantee that you and the audience will be comfortable (heat, AC, lights, noise).

Appearance

- Dress appropriately (usually one level above the audience).
- Remove any distracting jewelry, name tags, or badges before you start (it's all about you).
- Stand out from your backdrop (dress in contrasting colors so you don't disappear).
- Check yourself over in a mirror before you go on (lipstick, food in teeth, straighten tie, check zippers and buttons, etc.).

Food and Water

- Don't eat or drink anything that will detract from your presentation (no alcohol, etc.)
- Have a glass of water nearby (avoid dry lips, throat).

Be in the Know

- Read the local daily paper and listen to the news before you go (don't be the last to know; include appropriate late-breaking news or information in your presentation).

Equipment

- Know how to use the AV equipment (microphone, projector, VCR, etc.).
- Test out the mike beforehand to know how far to hold it from your mouth.
- Adjust mike so it does not hide your face.
- Ask to change the podium height if necessary.
- Do not assume that just because you have a loud voice that people will be able to hear you without a mike.
- Assume nothing will work the way it should—and plan accordingly (Murphy's Law).

Distractions

- Take steps to reduce or eliminate anything that might distract the audience from your presentation; this includes closing drapes or blinds so people are not tempted to look out the windows; leaving doors ajar so they won't make a noise when they are opened or closed; and asking the audience to turn off any cell phones and pagers (be sure to turn off yours as well).

Credibility

- Be believable (emphasize your credibility at the start of your presentation).
- Toot your own horn (write your own introduction to be read by the emcee).

Copies

- Bring an extra copy of your written introduction and your own remarks (just in case).

Demeanor

- Smile and act confident (look and act as though you are glad to be there).
- Be positive, upbeat and enthusiastic about your topic.

Content

- Prioritize and limit your messages (limit to three).
- Customize your presentation to meet the needs of the audience or organization.
- Answer the two key questions that every audience has of every speaker and every topic: (1) who cares? (2) why should I care?
- Make sure they understand you (refrain from using any jargon, buzzwords or technical terms or phrases that your audience may not understand).
- If on a panel, check with the other panelists beforehand to avoid repeating their points.

Rehearse

- Practice your presentation—but not to the point where it sounds memorized.

Don't Talk to Strangers

- Greet people as they arrive (this will guarantee that you will not be speaking to strangers, but rather to people you've just met).

Waiting to Go on

- Take one last bathroom break (better safe than sorry).
- While waiting to be introduced or if on a panel, do not look bored or distracted while others are speaking (pay attention).
- Remember that you are always on, even before you go on (everyone may be able to see what you are doing).

Notes

- Make sure any notes you need are legible, large, and easy to read in low light, and are in proper order.
- Number your notes or reference materials (in case you drop them or "gremlins" scramble them the night before).

Delivery

- Know how long you are expected to speak; be sure to give the audience a break every 75 minutes.
- Know your stuff (your material, arguments, facts, figures).

- Know what you will say to open and conclude your remarks, and eliminate any unnecessary information in between.
- Know how you will get and keep the audience's attention.
- Be sure to thank them for inviting you.
- Tell them why you are there (don't assume that they know).
- Show your story, don't just tell it (find and use charts, slides, etc.).
- Keep the audience awake (don't bore them).
- Don't get rattled if you forget some of your points; the audience will not know what you forgot to say.
- Finish your presentation no matter how bad you feel about it (the show must go on).
- Arrange for someone to give you a two-minute warning (don't speak longer than scheduled).
- Do not thank the audience for listening (it's demeaning to you and to them).
- Give the audience the gift of time (end early).
- Do not leave anything behind, such as speaking notes, remarks, or visuals (don't litter).

Humor

- Don't tell jokes unless you've already proven that you can tell jokes well (there's nothing funny about no one laughing at your jokes).

Visibility

- Make sure they can see you (don't hide behind podium).
- Do not hide your gestures (keep your hands up where the audience can see them).

Posture

- Maintain good posture when standing or sitting (no slouching).

Q&A Session

- Repeat the question before answering it so the audience can hear it.
- Respond honestly to questions (it's okay to say "I don't know").
- Don't allow one person to monopolize the session (let's meet afterwards).

- Summarize/rephrase lengthy questions for the audience.
- Do not allow Q&A session to drag on, and signal the audience that the session is almost over ("We have time for one more question").

Always Market Yourself

- Wear a company badge and REALTOR® pin if you are member of the National Association of REALTORS®.
- Bring a healthy supply of your business cards to hand out when necessary.

Seek Feedback

- Ask for feedback from the organizers about your speech, and modify your next presentation accordingly.

Study Others

- Pay attention to all speakers you see or hear in the future to help learn from their successes and avoid their failures.

Resources

To help sharpen your speaking skills:

- Join a local chapter of Toastmasters International (www.toastmasters.org).
- Take a public speaking class at your local college, university, or adult education center.

The Bottom Line

- Public speaking is an effective way to help publicize yourself to a variety of groups and organizations.
- There are several steps you can take to help ensure that your presentations are effective and successful.

How to Generate Publicity: Offer Your Perspectives on the Housing Market

Media Home Price Is Back Up: $971,500
Kathy Schlegel, president of the Marin Association of Realtors, said the June numbers "continue to show we still have a healthy, more balanced real estate market. We are seeing ... homes staying on the market longer and buyers don't feel the immediacy of having to make a fast purchase," Schlegel said. "they are looking at more homes before making their decision to buy."

Marin Independent Journal
San Rafael, Calif.
June 20, 2006

Advice and Insights: It is the job of journalists to report the facts of real estate-related stories, and not to inject their own opinions or predictions.

To help round out their stories, however, reporters will often seek out local real estate experts for their take on the housing market, the impact of interest rates on home buyers, etc. and include those comments in their stories.

Given how often news outlets do stories about the housing market, real estate professionals have many opportunities throughout the year to be quoted in the news about where they think the market is headed, the impact of prices and interest rates on consumers, etc.

Chapter 18

Timing is Everything

3 ... 2 ... 1

Timing is an important factor in determining whether and how much publicity a real estate agent can generate. This chapter explains the best months of the year, days of the week, and times of the day for attracting the attention of the general public and the media.

Trying to get the attention of the media to listen to your story is a lot like trying to have a conversation with somebody who's too busy at the time; there are times when you're more likely to have their undivided attention.

By waiting until their slow or quiet times, you'll increase the likelihood that journalists and your target audience will have the time, patience, and interest in your story and what you have to say about it.

Whatever you do, however, do not become a pest to reporters. If you leave three or four phone or e-mail messages with a reporter, editor, or columnist and they don't get back to you, then it's time to take the hint.

Here are some general guidelines for the best and worst times to call reporters.

Best

- Weekday mornings between 10 AM and noon, when most reporters and their editors arrive for work and are deciding which stories to cover that day.
- Earlier in the week rather than later, when reporters are in the initial stages of stories they may be working on for that week.

Worst

- Weekday afternoon after 4 PM, when most reporters are on deadline completing their stories.

- Any weekend.
- Any national or religious holiday.
- The days before or days after Thanksgiving or Christmas, or New Year's day, when they are most likely to take those days off.

Of course, these guidelines won't apply if you try to contact journalists in ways other than by phone, such as e-mail or fax.

Ironically, some of the best days and times to generate news coverage about yourself may be some of the worst days and times for reaching reporters: slow news days when there is less likely to be competing events or activities that vie for the media's attention, such as Fridays, weekends, and national holidays.

This is not to say that it is impossible to reach reporters during that time. Most news organizations have somebody on duty at all times, so if your news is important or urgent enough, you should be able to find somebody to talk to.

The Bottom Line

- Know the best and worst times to try to reach reporters.
- Don't be a pest: know when to give up with reporters who don't call you back.

How to Generate Publicity: Promote Performance and Sales Figures

Park Ave. Realtors Prospered In 2005

Park Avenue Realtors of Stroudsburg is celebrating its most successful year to date. "In 2005 our office exceeded $23 million in sales and individual realtors accomplished personal bests. This being my first year as broker, I couldn't be more pleased," said Broker/Owner Jean M. Lynch.

Pocono Record
March 30, 2006
Stroudsburg, Pa.

Advice and Insights: Most daily newspapers have business sections that cover the financial activities, successes, and failures of companies and organizations. These sections can provide your real estate company with the perfect forum to generate publicity about the success of your own business as measured in sales, and the number of listings, clients, or agents. Such stories can send important signals to consumers—and your competition—on how well you are doing in the marketplace.

While it is perfectly acceptable to release your own sales or other statistics to the local newspaper, you may get more media attention if that information comes from an industry-related group, organization, or publication, such as Real Trends:

REMAX Ocean Realty Ranks In Top 500

Real Trends, Inc., a national publishing and communications company that provides news, research and information-based services to the real estate industry, listed RE/MAX Ocean Realty as a Top 500 broker in the U.S. for 2005 based on sales volume. This is the third consecutive year RE/MAX has received this distinction, and is the only Outer Banks real estate firm included in the Top 500.

Outer Banks Sentinel
Aug. 19, 2006
Nags Head, N.C.

Chapter 19

Why Creativity Counts

But Don't Go Overboard

How real estate agents present themselves to the world helps shape how they are perceived by the public. This chapter shows some of the worst ways others have tried to capture the public's attention

Unless you're able to attract the attention of the media and the public, everything you say about your real estate services or expertise will fall on deaf ears.

Apparently working on the theory that different is better, some people seek attention by being as creative or unusual as possible, hoping that their efforts will stand out from the rest of the crowd. Sometimes they succeed—but for all the wrong reasons. That's because in their haste for news coverage, they may have forgotten some important principles—such as good taste, concern for the safety of others, attention to detail, and plain old common sense.

Here are a few examples of some of the best and worst ways people have tried to get the recognition they wanted:

In an effort to get the media to take notice of a news release announcing a client's blood-recycling machine that could help control blood-borne diseases such as AIDS, a public relations agency prepared and distributed a news release about the equipment splattered with fake blood.

The release certainly got the attention of at least one news organization. *The Wall Street Journal* ran a story about it with this headline: "'Bloody' Gimmick of PR Firm Leaves Some Seeing Red." The article was about the negative reaction many people had to the stunt and how, in the minds of health officials and public relations experts, using fake blood to get the attention of the press was offensive and in bad taste.

Some attention-getting stunts and promotions are better left on the drawing board. This was the case when a disc jockey in Fort Worth, Texas announced on the air that the radio station's staff had hidden $5 and $10 bills in books located in the fiction section of a local public library.

But the radio station, which wanted to use the stunt to help boost public interest in the library, had not bothered to tell the library's staff about the promotion.

Imagine the staff's surprise when 500 people rushed through the doors of the library, stampeded through the book stacks and proceeded to open, tear, destroy, and toss 3,000 books on the floor as they desperately looked for the money.

The radio station apologized for the stunt and donated $10,000 to the library to help pay for the damage it had caused.

The Bottom Line

- How you present yourself to the public can help determine how you are perceived.

- There are some lines you should not cross in your efforts to publicize yourself or your company.

How to Generate Publicity: Ride Another's Coattails

Fame and Fries
Diane Carpenter isn't so hot on McDonald's. But the Santa Rosa real estate agent adores the TV commercial wherein a handsome young [McDonald's] customer tosses so much change into a can on a bookshelf that the shelf collapses. The fellow is Diane's son ..."

Press Democrat
July 9, 2006
Santa Rosa, Calif.

Advice and Insights: Most of the examples in this book are about the publicity real estate professionals have received about their activities, accomplishments, or expertise.

Occasionally, however, there may be opportunities for the media to do stories about you simply because of your relationship to someone else. Sometime, the news angle or story angle may be about a part of your life that has nothing to do with real estate.

Since these "coattail" stories will usually have limited interest to local news organizations, it is not necessary to prepare or distribute a full-blown news releases about your role or relationship to something or someone else.

Instead, contact the news editor, tell them about the story angle, and ask which reporter or columnist might be interested in doing a story about it. If interested, the journalist will likely want to do a phone interview with you to get the information they need for the story.

Chapter 20

How to Understand and Get Along with the Media

They Don't Have Horns or Eat Their Young

Discusses the 19 best ways to understand and work with editors and reporters, and which strategies and tactics are likely to be most effective in convincing them to do stories about a real estate agent or broker.

An important part of any effort to generate publicity about yourself or your real estate company is a basic understanding of the media, and how to get along with editors and reporters.

First and foremost, it is important to realize that reporters are looking to satisfy their own needs, not yours. They wear the shoes of their readers, viewers, or listeners. While you may have a burning desire to tell them all about your real estate services and expertise, their task is to gather as much information as possible and produce a story that will hold an audience's attention. *Like you, they are storytellers* (see Chapter 8*). They are looking for great anecdotes and simple explanations.*

Reality Check

Boiled down to the essentials, the strategies and tactics that are most likely to result in the stories you want about yourself or your company can be summarized by the following "key truths" about working with the media, and discussed in greater depth or detail throughout the book.

1. Reporters and columnists are neither your friends nor your enemies. They are professionals just like you, and are trying to do the best job they can.

2. Don't ask reporters to do a story about you. Give them reasons why they should.

3. Be brief. The average sound bite is about seven seconds long (and shrinking). If you cannot answer a reporter's question in the time it takes to read this paragraph aloud, it is unlikely your response will be used by television or radio reporters.

4. Prioritize the three most important things you would like to see in the newspaper about yourself or company, and keep your remarks focused on those points.

5. Reporters will always ask the one question that you don't want to answer.

6. The most important thing you can tell a reporter about your story is who will care and why.

7. Most reporters hate it when you call them to find out if they received the news release you sent them. But most of them will appreciate it if you let them know ahead of time that you are sending them a story you think they will be interested in covering.

8. The easiest way to find out what stories reporters are most interested in covering is to ask them, and study the stories they've already done.

9. There is no such thing as being too prepared for a media interview.

10. Assume that everything you tell a reporter is on the record and may be used in their story.

11. If you don't know the answer to a reporter's question, say so. Then tell him or her you will find out the answer and call back as soon as possible.

12. Ask reporters what you can do to help make their job easier.

13. Never call a reporter when he or she is on deadline.

14. Never assume that your press list is accurate, complete, or up to date.

15. Never be a pain to a reporter. But always be a resource of information.

16. The day a reporter sends you a copy of his story for your review is the day you will win the lottery.

17. The best way to help ensure that a reporter will use your press release is to write it as though it's a newspaper story.

18. Media interviews can be similar to auditions. Once a reporter knows you are reliable and dependable, he or she is likely to call again.

19. When a reporter does agree to interview you for a story, he or she will usually assume that you will answer questions they ask. If there are issues that you do not want to discuss or queries that you'd rather avoid, it's best that you have a clear understanding with the reporter beforehand about the

topics he wants to discuss. Otherwise, you may be better off not doing the interview in the first place. Of course, in your efforts to protect yourself, you also run the risk of offending the reporter, who may decide to simply not do the interview.

Karen Friedman, a former TV reporter in Philadelphia, observes that "the real rub between journalists and business is that many business people are afraid that reporters will go for the jugular or the negative. As a reporter, I often found that businesspeople were afraid of me and not always ready to provide the kind of information I was looking for. Many business executives think reporters have a hidden agenda. We don't. Reporters are just looking for the information they need to do their job."

Hall of Shame

When giving radio or television interviews, always assume that the microphone is on and that every word you say may be recorded or broadcast.

Then-Maryland State Senate President Thomas V. "Mike" Miller, Jr. found this out the hard way when he used profanities to describe Baltimore and its economic problems during an interview with a reporter from a Washington television station. The station did not delete his colorful remarks from the story, and several newspapers included the expletives in its coverage about the incident.

Miller later said he had no idea that that everything he told the reporter would be recorded or might be broadcast—even though he was wearing a microphone, had gone through voice-level checks, and bright television lights were trained on him at the time.

Miller apologized for what he described as his "inappropriate and unsavory" remarks.

Every so often a reporter is caught making a similar gaffe. While attending an event at which President George W. Bush was delivering a speech, CNN reporter Kyra Phillips forgot to turn off her microphone while talking in a bathroom. Her comments were carried live over the network while the president gave his speech.

Phillips, who apparently had a sense of humor about her snafu, went on the David Letterman Show to give her top ten excuses for what happened:

10. "Still haven't mastered complicated On/Off switch."

9. "Larry King told me he does this all the time."

8. "How was I supposed to know we had a reporter embedded in the bathroom?"

7. "I honestly never knew this sort of thing was frowned upon."

6. "Couldn't resist chance to win $10,000 on 'America's Funniest Home Videos'."

5. "I was set up by those bastards at Fox News."

4. "Oh, like *you've* never gone to the bathroom and had it broadcast on national television!"

3. "I just wanted that hunky Lou Dobbs to notice me."

2. "OK, so I was drunk and couldn't think straight."

1. "You have to admit, it made the speech a lot more interesting."

The Bottom Line

- Reporters are just trying to do the best jobs they can.
- Journalists are not your friends—or your enemies.
- You will likely have better working relationships with reporters if you know how they work and what's important to them.

How to Generate Publicity: Make Predictions or Forecasts

Columbia Housing Market Overbuilt
Columbia has too many new homes on the market, which some builders and
Realtors say might force anxious builders to cut prices ... Realtor Carl Freiling,
who mainly works in Ashland and southern Boone County, said the problem there
only began around late May ... He predicts that, like Columbia, the number of
new home permits will decline and buyers will return. "At a certain point, folks get
over their jitters," Freiling said. "It will take a matter of months, not years."

Columbia Missourian
Aug. 7, 2006
Columbia, Mo.

Advice and Insights: Although reporters will not make their own predictions
about real estate trends or developments in the stories they write, they will often
include forecasts that are made by real estate professionals. If you are sure that
your crystal ball is in working order, then sharing your predictions with the local
real estate reporter can be an effective way to generate the publicity you want.

Chapter 21

What to Do or Say Before, During, or After You Meet the Media

Your Checklist for Interview Success

> This chapter lists 64 ways to help guarantee that the interviews you do with reporters are productive and successful, to ensure your quotes are more likely to be used by journalists in their stories, and make sure that the media does an accurate job of reporting.

The news release you wrote and sent to your media list was well received, and a reporter has just called to interview you.

Like most people, your first reaction may be: What am I going to do now?

First, remain calm.

Second, congratulate yourself on your efforts to convince a reporter to do a story. Now it's time to take steps to ensure that:

- The interview is successful.

- Your quotes are used.

- The story is accurate.

While there are a lot of things you should do, there are many things you should not do. One of the most important things to avoid at all costs is to agree to do an interview with the reporter right then and there. Instead, try to delay the interview until you've had enough time (whether it's a few minutes or a few hours) to properly prepare for it.

You'd never think to show a home or other property to a client without first learning something about their preferences and needs, would you? Of course not.

It's the same principle when it comes to meeting with the media. The more you know before you enter an interview situation, the better off you'll be. You can also decide whether you even want to do the interview in the first place.

Most reporters will understand it if you say you're busy just then, but promise that you will call back in a few minutes for the interview. Take that time (or more if you can get it) to review the guidelines and suggestions on the following interview checklist.

Interview Checklist
Topic

- What is the topic and focus of the story? (Try to have the reporter narrow it down as much as possible.)
- Can the reporter share with you the list of questions he or she plans to ask?
- Based on the answers to the questions listed above, is this an interview that you really want to do or should agree to do? Are you the best person to do this interview? If not, refer the reporter to the appropriate individual in your company or to one of your colleagues.

Deadline

- When does the reporter want to do the interview?
- Can you call him/her back later for the interview?

The Reporter

- For which news organization does the reporter work?
- Who is their audience?
- How much time does the reporter need for the interview?
- Have you sent the reporter relevant background information he/she needs prior to the interview, such as a copy of your news release, fact sheet, or press kit?
- Has the reporter received and read the information you sent?
- Who else is the reporter talking to for the story?
- Can you research other stories the reporter has done before you do the interview?

Your Message

- What is the overarching message you want to communicate in the interview?
- What are the three most important points you want to make?
- Do you have the latest information about the topic?
- Have you practiced your answers?
- What visuals can you use to help show your story?

General Interview Guidelines
Length

- Set a time limit on all interviews: 15 to 20 minutes for most interviews
- Keep your answers short: 20 to 30 seconds for print interviews, 10 to 20 seconds for radio and television.

Questions

- Anticipate all questions the reporter might ask: the good, the bad, and the ugly.
- Put yourself in the shoes of the reporter. If you were the journalist, what questions would you ask?

Setting

- If the interview will be held in your office, make sure any papers or information you don't want the reporter to see have been put safely away; let your colleagues know that a reporter will be in the office so they can act accordingly.
- If the interview will be conducted over the phone, make sure there are no distracting noises that will break your concentration, or that may be picked up by the phone.
- If the interview will be done online or through a series of exchanged e-mails, be sure to read the questions and your responses carefully before hitting the "send" button. This includes doing a spell check of your response and reading your answer aloud to see if it sounds as good as it looks.

Answers

- Have an appropriate answer ready for each possible question.

- Have immediate access to all the information you'll need to answer the questions.
- Customize your answers for the audience of the news organization.
- Tell the truth and keep your answers consistent, no matter how many times you are interviewed.
- Find ways to repeat your key points throughout the interview.
- Assume *everything* you tell the reporter is on the record.
- Be prepared to cite the source of any studies, statistics, etc. that you may use in your answers.
- If you don't know the answer to a question, say so. Then tell the reporter you will have to call them back with an answer.
- Use bridging techniques to avoid giving a direct answer to a question you don't want to answer. Jump from the question he asks to the one you want to answer by saying: "That's an interesting question, but a more important question is …" Then ask and answer your own question.
- Explain why you can't give information requested by a reporter or answer a particular question.
  For example: I'd be glad to share this month's sales figures, but the information will not be available until next week. I will call you when the report is released. .
- Don't repeat a negative question as part of your answer; repeating negative words in your answer could be used in a headline.
  Question: How long will the depression in the housing market last?
  Bad Answer: The depression will last through the end of the year. (Possible headline based on this response: REALTOR® Predicts Housing Depression to Continue)
  Better Answer: Our market is finally returning to normal, and we are seeing a much more balanced market than we've had in quite some time. I expect this balanced market to continue through next year (Possible headline based on this response: REALTOR® Says Balanced Market Will Continue).

Don't:

- Answer a question unless you understand what is being asked. If necessary, ask the reporter to repeat or explain the question, or rephrase the question in your own words.
- Expect the reporter to ask you the questions you want to answer. Look for ways to include in your answer the points you want to make.

- Answer hypothetical questions.
- Get mad, defensive, or argue with the reporter.
- Say "no comment." Instead, explain why you cannot or will not answer a question.
- Talk longer than you have to in order to answer the question.
- Use lots of numbers or statistics in your answers; use them sparingly in order to make your point.
- Agree to talk "off the record".
- Criticize your competition.
- Use jargon, technical terms, or acronyms in your answers.

Listen

- Listen to what the reporter is saying, and pay attention to how the reporter is reacting to your answers.
- Don't assume you know what the reporter is asking before he or she finishes the question. Be sure you listen and fully understand the question before responding.

Voice

- Use a conversational tone—don't give a speech.
- Avoid speaking in a monotone.

Body Language (for in-person interviews)

- Maintain good posture.
- Smile.
- Use appropriate gestures to express yourself.
- Maintain appropriate eye contact with the reporter.
- Don't fidget in your seat or do anything that will distract the reporter from your answer.

Attire

- Dress appropriately for in-person interviews.

Feedback

- Tape record your answers for later reference and evaluation. Don't record the reporter without his/her consent.

Attitude

- Appear friendly, confident, and upbeat.
- Be positive, upbeat, enthusiastic, and confident in your answers and demeanor.
- Be yourself as much as you can. Project self-confidence in the way you dress, your body language, and the tone and manner of your voice.
- Appear eager to give honest answers.

After the Interview: How Did You Do?

- Being as objective as possible, evaluate how the interview went and ask yourself what you would do differently the next time.
- If you tape recorded your answers, listen to your responses to make sure you gave the answer you wanted in the most effective way possible. Based on what you hear, how would you respond to the same question the next time?
- When the story with your interview is printed or broadcast, evaluate the story to see how your interview was used. Did the reporter accurately report your answers? Are there any mistakes or errors in the story that you should call to the attention of the reporter or editor?
- Send a letter or e-mail to the reporter to thank him or her for the interview, and offer to be of assistance on future stories.

Exercise: Play Reporter

Before you are interviewed by a reporter, take the time to ask questions by the toughest journalist in the world: you. Since you are (or should be) intimately familiar with every detail and nuance of your story, you are also in the best position to come up with the most difficult or embarrassing questions a reporter might ask.

In this exercise, put yourself in the shoes of the reporter and ask yourself all the possible questions he or she might pose to you in a real interview. For example, let's assume that a reporter wants to interview you about the local housing market. Here are some of the questions he or she might ask during the interview, followed by examples of possible responses.

Your answers, of course, should reflect your own opinions and observations about the local market at the time of the interview and incorporate the key messages you want to communicate to the public (see Chapter 10). The following mock interview is for illustration purposes only.

Reporter:	How is the market doing lately?
You:	The local housing market has really cooled off, and is the slowest I've seen in the ten years that I've been in real estate.
Reporter:	Is this true for all types of housing in our area?
You:	It is an across-the-board slow-down that affects new and existing homes, condos, and town houses.
Reporter:	Do you have any facts or research to support that?
You:	Yes, the latest figures from the National Association of REALTORS® show a similar cooling down of the market, and I will be glad to send those reports to you if you'd like.
Reporter:	What impact are interest rates having on buyers?
You:	Interest rates appear to be holding steady and don't seem to be much of a factor right now.
Reporter:	How much longer do you think the housing market will be like this?
You:	I wish I had a crystal ball, but I don't. We will just have to wait and see how things go on a month-by-month basis.
Reporter:	What advice do you have for people who are thinking of selling their homes?

You: Take steps now to get your house ready to put
                              on the market. This includes making needed
                              repairs, giving your property as much curb
                              appeal as possible, and working with your
                              REALTOR® to set an appropriate listing price.

After filling in the blanks, read your own responses out loud. Then ask
yourself:

1. Are your answers short enough? (See Chapter 22)

2. Do your answers use any of the sound bite techniques outlined in
   Chapter 22?

3. How will you feel if you see these comments in the newspaper?

If you are not satisfied with your answers to the reporter's possible questions,
continue to revise and practice your responses until you are satisfied.

Hall of Shame: Learning the Hard Way

As strange as it may seem, it is possible to be interviewed by a reporter without
your knowledge or consent.

Nancy Kervin worked as a research assistant at *Congressional Quarterly*, a non-
partisan magazine which reports on the activities of Congress. Her responsibili-
ties included responding to telephone inquiries from subscribers and the media.

One day an Associated Press reporter called seeking information about the voting
record of Rep. Bob Edgar (D-Pa), who was running for the U. S. Senate at the time.
Asked how Edgar's voting record compared with other members of the House of
Representatives, Kervin said, "This year, he's definitely in the basement."

It was not until later that Kervin discovered she had done more than simply
provide information to the reporter: she had also been interviewed and all of her
comments were on the record. The realization came when her boss received an
angry phone call from Edgar's office, which had read her following comments in
a story about the Senate campaign in the *Harrisburg Patriot* newspaper:

"According to *Congressional Quarterly*, a Washington-based political journal,
Edgar missed 39 percent of the votes taken from Jan. 1 to Aug. 20. "This year,
he's definitely in the basement," said a research staffer for the magazine."

Edgar's office demanded to know why a member of the magazine's staff was
making editorial comments about the lawmaker's voting record to the media.
Kervin was counseled by her supervisor about her remarks and told not to share
her personal opinions with reporters.

As Kervin observed later, "I learned the hard way to keep your opinions to yourself, and that you should always assume that anything you tell a reporter may wind up in his story."

The Bottom Line

- Be prepared before you contact a reporter.
- Before any interview, practice answering all potential questions.
- Assume that everything you tell a reporter is "on the record."

How to Generate Publicity: Issue a Call to Action

Area Needs to Court Developers: Realtor
Columbus needs a breath of fresh air in the housing market—and fast—says local real estate agent Doris Hardy. Hardy says Columbus needs several developments totaling in the range of 400 homes.

Columbus Dispatch
June 30, 2006
Columbus, Ohio

Advice and Insights: If you think your community needs something—whether it's more housing, police, firefighters, stoplights, etc.—speak up and tell local editors and reporters about your concerns. Your call for action to help address a local problem or issue may spark a journalist's interest in doing a story about it.

A news release about your call to action can help demonstrate your concern about the matter, attract attention to the situation, and result in positive publicity for you and your company.

Often, REALTOR® associations ask their own members to help address an important local problem, while generating publicity about their concerns. To wit:

Group Joins Mosquito Breeding Site Hunt
The Arizona Association of Realtors is asking members to report abandoned or poorly maintained pools to Maricopa County, in an effort to reduce mosquito breeding sites during the West Nile virus season.

East Valley Tribune
July 23, 2004
Phoenix, Ariz.

Chapter 22

What You Need to Know about Sound Bites

The Magic 7 Seconds

Unless you can summarize your story in seven seconds or less, your quotes will be left on the cutting room floor; this chapter lists guidelines to prepare sound and ink bites so reporters will be more likely to include them in their stories.

Summarizing the impact of rising home prices on consumers, Barry Crotty, a real estate agent who was then with Pacific Union in Greenbrae, Calif., told the *Marin Independent Journal*: "The bottom line is that buyers still want value, so they're becoming less frenzied as the prices have gone up and up. They're willing to wait while they're looking for the needle in the haystack."

If you are like most people, you can talk for at least a few minutes on any number of topics, whether it's about a favorite DVD, Web site, or recent client. But when you have an opportunity to be interviewed by a reporter, it doesn't matter how long you can talk. Can you, as Crotty did, boil down your opinions, observations, accomplishments, or activities to seven seconds, or about 35 words?

Seven seconds is not a lot of time. (How long is it? Count out loud from 1,001 to 1,007 to see for yourself, or time yourself against a watch with a second hand.) But seven seconds is often all the time a television or radio station may give you in an edited on-air story to talk about your activity or accomplishment, make a statement, give a comment, or react to a news announcement.

These brief remarks are known as sound bites—small portions or "bites" from interviews that are inserted in news stories—to enliven or illustrate news reports. Ink bites, the printed version of sound bites, can range from five to 50 words. As a general rule of thumb, if your response to a reporter's question runs longer than the time it takes to read this sentence aloud, most reporters won't use your quote in their stories. Instead, they will likely condense, paraphrase, or ignore your answer entirely.

Sound bites were not always so short. In the 1960s, news programs often allowed people to talk for up to 45 seconds at a time. But three factors helped to shorten sound bites:

1. Pressures on local television stations and national networks to make more money, which led them to sell more advertising time for their news programs.

2. The proliferation of multiple news outlets for consumers to choose from, ranging from cable channels to Web sites.

3. The effect of MTV's popular high-energy, fast-paced programming, which catered to the short attention spans of youthful audiences.

Faced with the challenge to sell more advertising, attract and keep the attention of viewers, and stay competitive in a crowded media market, broadcast executives began to produce shorter, more visually appealing stories with sound bites to match. It's these same pressures that are forcing the length of sound bites to shrink a bit more with every passing year.

By definition, any sound bite or ink bite is a good one since it means you said something interesting and short enough to be included in a reporter's story. But good is not good enough. Your comments should also help generate the news coverage you want by meeting the following nine criteria:

1. Creates or enhances the reputation you want.

2. Places you in the best possible light.

3. Conveys the message you want to send to the public.

4. Accurately captures the essence of what you want to say on the topic.

5. Feels right or comfortable for you to say.

6. Offends no one.

7. Is credible and believable.

8. Is interesting enough to encourage the reporter and other members of the media to call on you for future interviews.

9. Is brief and to the point.

With so much riding on what you say to the media and how you say it, the ability to prepare and deliver effective sound bites is one of the most important skills you can have. The challenge is to provide journalists with quotes they can use while serving your best interests at the same time.

You can learn a lot about sound bites by reading about, listening to, and watching speeches and media interviews with politicians. That's because most politicians do an excellent job of preparing and delivering sound bites to help win votes, explain their stands on issues or advocate causes—just as you need to promote your own activities, accomplishments, services, or expertise.

Television and radio news broadcasts and newspaper and magazine articles are full of sound bites and ink bites from people in different professions and walks of life. Studying what these newsmakers say and how they say it is one of the best continuing educations you can obtain in the art of preparing and delivering sound bites.

After preparing hundreds of quotes for clients and studying thousands of sound bites over the years, I've come to the conclusion that effective sound bites are like sandwiches: there are thousands of ways to make them according to your own tastes and preferences.

The sound bite recipes you use will depend on what you want to say, how you want to say it, and what you want to accomplish with your remarks. Since quotes can make or break reputations—and sometimes careers—you should choose your words carefully and organize your thoughts before you are interviewed by the media.

Although there are no guarantees journalists will include the quotes you want in their stories, you can certainly stack the deck in your favor by using one or more of these sound bite techniques:

Technique	Example
Clichés	"Today's buyers are a day late and a dollar short."
Absolutes	"This is our best year ever."
Analogies	"Finding a home in today's market is like a game of musical chairs."
Personal Experience	"I'm having my best year ever."
Colorful Phrases	"It's a feeding frenzy out there."
Predictions	"The market will continue to cool down for at least the next six months."
Anecdotes	"A funny thing happened to me at a recent open house …"
Warnings	"Unless sellers lower their asking prices, buyers will continue to stay away."
Rhetorical questions	"How high is high?"

Exercise: Write Your Own Sound Bite

With the possible exception of politicians, it is almost impossible for most people to come up with the perfect sound bite without some degree of preparation and practice. So before you're asked to deliver your first pithy seven-second sound bite by a television reporter, take a few minutes to go through the following exercise.

1. In 50 words or so, describe the benefits and advantages of your company, organization, services, or expertise.

2. Now, go over what you just wrote and eliminate any jargon, buzzwords, or other language that may be unfamiliar to the general public or your target audience. Keep the language simple and basic. Take a look at the recipes for the most successful sound bites earlier in this chapter and use at least one of them in your description.

3. It's time now to shrink your words to a manageable sound bite length (about seven seconds or so). Rewrite your description one more time, but this time keep the length to no more than 50 words.

4. We're almost done. Take a long hard look at the 50 words you just wrote, and try to say the same thing in 20 words or less. Remember to include at least one of the "sound bite ingredients" from earlier in this chapter.

5. Now it's time for the acid test. Ask a friend, colleague, or family member to play the role of a television reporter, and have them ask you the following question:

6. "Tell me about your (service) (company) (expertise)."

7. Now, give them your sound bite.

8. Finally, ask the "reporter" what he or she thought of your answer.

9. Was your sound bite interesting? Was it short enough? Did it capture the attention of the reporter? Did it adequately convey enough information in order to provide the audience with a good idea of the benefits and advantages of your company, services, or expertise?

10. If not, go back and read this chapter again and try this exercise one more time.

Just as an athlete does warm-up exercises before a game or race, you should do these warm-up sound bite exercises several hours or days before your interviews with the media. Make a list of the three most important points you want to make during the interview, as well as a list of every possible question you think you could be asked, and prepare an appropriate sound bite response to each of them.

The more you practice, the more real and natural your sound bite will sound, and the less you have to worry about condensing the most important parts of your story down to the magic seven seconds.

The Bottom Line

- Help ensure your comments are used by reporters by limiting the length of your responses to their questions.
- There are sound bite techniques you can use to help ensure your quotes are included in a journalist's story.

How to Generate Publicity: Conduct Workshops

Home Buyers Get Tools for Finding Homes
The husband and wife realtor team of Robert and Victorine Clarke held the first of its home-buying seminars last week as part of an effort to help local residents of the Bowie and Lanham communities to take advantage of what they say is now a buyers' market.

The Prince George's Sentinel
June 29, 2006
Seabrook, Md.

Advice and Insights: Some agents do more than just list properties or represent buyers—they help educate consumers about buying or selling real estate. If you have knowledge you're willing to share with the public and have the necessary public speaking and teaching skills to do it, holding seminars and workshops in your community can be a good marketing tactic and the basis for positive publicity.

Chapter 23

Help Guarantee the Success of Your Publicity Efforts

Don't Be a Victim of Murphy's Law

The chapter explains 15 things that can go wrong when real estate agents deal with the media and the steps agents and brokers can take to ensure their stories are read, seen, or heard by the public.

Murphy's Law says that "anything that can wrong will go wrong." The corollary to the law is that "Murphy was an optimist."

Here is a list of the 15 things that will most likely go astray when you deal with the media. The more precautions you take to avoid these mishaps, the less likely they are to happen as you seek to generate publicity for yourself or your company.

1. It isn't clear how your story affects audiences of the news organizations that received your news release.

2. Your story was not packaged or presented as a legitimate news story.

3. You are not promoting the most interesting or newsworthy aspects of your story.

4. You did not include relevant facts, figures, or background information that is important to your story.

5. Your news release was too long or the headline did not grab the attention of the reporter.

6. You sent out your release on a busy news day and it couldn't compete for coverage against the scheduled events and announcements made by other individuals, organizations, or corporations.

7. You didn't have any visuals to help show your story, or the visuals you did have weren't interesting enough.

8. You couldn't explain or tell your story effectively to the reporters.

9. You didn't identify or target the news organizations that would have been most interested in your story.

10. Your media lists were outdated or inaccurate.

11. You sent your news release to the wrong editors or reporters.

12. You waited too long to return a reporter's phone call.

13. You did a poor job of answering a reporter's questions.

14. You didn't provide the reporter with the additional information he requested.

15. You didn't show why people should care about your story.

The Bottom Line

- Many things can go wrong when you work with the media.
- Preparation is an important key to success.

How to Generate Publicity: Move Your Office

Prudential Stedman & Associates Realtors Relocate To Downtown
A chance to occupy one of the best corners in Natchez was too good to let pass, said husband and wife Joe and Sue Stedman of Prudential Stedman & Associate Realtors. Work is underway at 112 Main St., where the ground floor space will become the new home of the Stedman Company.

The Natchez Democrat
Jan. 15, 2005
Natchez, Miss.

Advice and Insights: To the uninitiated, having the paper write a story about the fact you are moving may be hard to believe. After all, who could possibly care?

But the truth of the matter is that some publications do care.

By studying the stories that are carried by your local news outlets, you will a better idea about the types of stories they like to cover. Granted, the article you get may not be very long, but a small story is better than no story at all.

Chapter 24

What to Do When News Organizations Make Mistakes

Don't Take it Laying Down

> This chapter looks at the 15 most common reporting mistakes and four ways to correct them.

Reporters produce anywhere from a handful to hundreds of stories every year, so it is inevitable that they occasionally get something wrong in their stories. But even if journalists make mistakes less than one percent of the time, think of all the stories that are wrong in some way.

For example, here's a correction that a major daily newspaper published concerning a mistake made by one of their columnists:

> Norma Adams-Wada's June 15 column incorrectly called Mary Ann Thompson-Frank a socialist. She is a socialite.

Dallas Morning News (Source: Regrettheerror.com)

What can possibly go wrong when a reporter prepares a story based on an interview with you? Plenty.

The list of potential mistakes includes:

- Reporting what you said.
- Reporting or describing what you did.
- Your name or the names of others who are mentioned or quoted in the story.
- The name of your company, division, or organization.
- Web site addresses.

- Phone numbers, fax numbers, or e-mail addresses.
- Job titles.
- Your age, sex, race, or physical description.

But even if the reporter gets those basics, there are plenty of other details he can get wrong.

They include:

- The name or description of your real estate services.
- The date, time, location, or details of an event or activity.
- Facts, figures, and statistics.
- Conclusions, projections or forecasts.
- Interpretation or analysis of the information you gave him.
- The photo or illustration that accompanies your article.
- The caption or cut lines that describe the picture or illustration.

In short, any aspect of the story is subject to error.

What can you do when the media makes these or other mistakes?

Everything you can, as soon as you can do it.

While it's impossible to unring a bell that has been rung, it is possible—and important—that you take steps to have an error in a story corrected as soon as possible. When the media makes a mistake, you should:

- Call the reporter who did the story and explain the error.
- If you can't reach the reporter right away, ask to speak to an editor about the matter.
- Ask that a correction be printed or broadcast as soon as possible.
- Monitor the news organization to ensure they make the correction.

PR Week, an industry publication, recommends against shooting from the hip or lip when a mistake occurs. Instead, plan a strategy and resist the urge to act on impulse. If you think the matter may lead to a legal action against the news organization, don't contact the reporter until you've had a chance to speak to an attorney.

When called to their attention, newspapers will usually print a correction the next day, and magazines may run a clarification in their next issue.

You have to act fast, however, if the mistake is broadcast on television or radio. If you hurry and call the station immediately, sometimes they will announce the correction during the same newscast or make note of it on the next broadcast.

Resources

To keep up on the latest mistakes that are made by the media, and what they've done to correct them, go to www.regrettheerror.com.

The Bottom Line

- Like everyone else, reporters make mistakes.
- There are steps you can take to help prevent or correct those mistakes.

How to Generate Publicity: Sponsor Events and Projects

A Traveling (Soccer) Man
Starting a fledging travel soccer squad was not a shoot-at-the-hip decision. There was a multitude of hurdles to jump. "We needed a sponsor to make it affordable," [Gino] DiNardo said. "We needed jerseys and there were fees to pay." Stepping up to provide the needed funds was realtor Cenorina Reyes of Realty World Caton Crossing. "This could not have happened without our sponsor," DiNardo said.

The Herald News
July 22, 2006
Joliet, Ill.

Advice and Insights: Sponsoring appropriate projects and activities in the community can be great backdrops against which real estate agents or brokers can seek to build or reinforce name recognition for themselves while generating news coverage about their company, expertise, or accomplishments.

Public awareness about your generosity or community spirit does not have to end after the event does. Be sure to include copies of any stories or mentions of your support in presentations and other marketing materials, and on your Web site (see Part V for more ideas on getting the most out of your publicity).

These sponsorships also provide important networking opportunities with local community and business leaders, government officials, and concerned residents—all of whom can be sources for leads, listings, or sales.

Chapter 25

Why and How You Should Be a Resource to Editors, Reporters, and Columnists

It's Not Who You Know, but Who Knows about You

This chapter shows five steps you can take to ensure that reporters know about and can contact you for interviews.

There are usually two reasons why a reporter will want to talk to you: either because of something you sent him or her, or the fact that you may have information or insights the reporter needs for his or her story.

Obviously, if you sent the reporter a news release, he'd know how to contact you for an interview (assuming, of course, you included your phone number or e-mail address).

But what if a reporter is working on a real estate-related topic in which you have some valuable knowledge or expertise, but doesn't know you even exist or how to reach you to arrange an interview.

The answer is for you to become a resource of information to as many editors, reporters, and columnists as possible so that they will know who you are, your areas of real estate expertise, your qualifications, and how to contact you.

The best ways to become a resource to the media are to:

- Find out which editors, reporters, and columnists cover the topics in which you have knowledge or expertise and target those news organizations you think would be interested in interviewing you at some point. One of the best ways to do this is call the news organization and ask the operator or news assignment editor which journalist to contact about what you have to say. Or, many news organizations now post on their Web sites a list of reporters and the topics they cover, along with e-mail addresses and other contact information.

- Send them a letter, memo, or e-mail describing your background, areas of expertise and, a list of the topics about which you can discuss.

- Don't be shy. If necessary, call the news organization and ask the operator or assignment desk which reporter covers the topics that concern you. Or ask the editors to send your information to the reporters who cover those subjects.

- Subscribe to a service such as ProfNet (see resources section below), which will notify you when reporters are seeking interviews or information for their stories. If you have what the journalists are looking for on a particular topic, they will contact you for more information or to arrange to talk with you.

- Give good quotes. Reporters are often inclined to interview people who they know can give provide quotes. When reporters see that you've been quoted by one news organization, for example, they may seek to contact you for interviews for their own stories. Consider your quotes to be as much a marketing opportunity to promote yourself to the media as they are a way to promote yourself or company to the public.

Resources

The following Web sites or services can help promote you as a resource to editors and reporters and locate reporters who may be interested in doing stories about you or your real estate company:

- www.Yearbooknews.com.
- www.rtir.com.
- www.ProfNet.com.

The Bottom Line

- It may be impossible to know all the reporters in your city or region.
- Take steps to let journalists know about your areas of expertise, and how they can reach you for interviews.

How to Generate Publicity: Capitalize on Your Hobbies and Sidelines

Realtor Tests Mettle with Adventure Racing
Beau Beau Mooneyham methodically juggles his life, career and direction. "You have to keep going. You can't put things off," Mooneyham says on a break between a gig mowing lawns for his dad's handyman business and a home inspection for a property he's selling as a Realtor for Murney Associates. Both jobs fit his affinity for adventure racing. While building his career as a Realtor one home sale at a time and helping his dad, Mooneyham continues to race in 10 to 12 triathlons, road races and adventure races a year; some are qualifiers for the USARA Adventure Race National Championship.

New Leader
Aug. 3, 2006
Springfield, Mo.

Advice and Insights: Like many people, you may have a hobby or vocation that helps to take your mind off your day job. If you enjoy unusual or offbeat activities or projects, they may be the perfect fodder to help attract a journalist in doing a story about you or your company.

Chapter 26

Why and How You Should Study the Media

Reduce Your Learning Curve

This chapter explains how to use news outlets as a continuing education class about the media and how to take advantage of that knowledge.

There's an easy, effective, and affordable way to find out what kind of stories media outlets will cover, the types of quotes they like to use, or how your competition is being portrayed by different news organizations.

All you have to do is:

- Read a local or national newspaper.
- Subscribe to a newsletter or magazine that covers the real estate industry.
- Watch the local and national news.
- Listen to news reports on your radio.
- Surf the Internet.
- Do a keyword search on a computer database.

Too busy to read everything or follow everything you should? Then you can subscribe to Google to receive free alerts when stories are done on the topics or keywords you specify.

To get the most insight about the media from your research, look for the following "clues":

Print Stories

- How long are the stories?

- In what part of the publication do they appear (business, lifestyle, sports, or the front news section)?
- How often do they include quotes?
- Who appears to be quoted more often, and why?
- How long are their quotes and what do you think of what they said?
- If you had been interviewed for the same story, what would you have told the reporter?
- What kind of pictures do they use (color, black-and-white, head-and - shoulder shots, etc.)?
- Whose byline usually appears above the stories that are of most interest to you?

Television Stories

- How long are the stories?
- What time or in what part of the newscast did the story air?
- How often do they include interviews?
- Who appears to be quoted more often, and why?
- How long are their quotes and what do you think of what they said?
- If you had been interviewed for the same story, what would you have told the reporter?
- What kind of pictures do they show during the story?
- What is the name of the reporter who covered the story?

Radio Stories

- How long are the stories?
- What time or in what part of the newscast did the story air?
- How often do they include interviews?
- Who appears to be quoted more often, and why?
- How long are their quotes, and what do you think of what they said?
- If you had been interviewed for the same story, what would you have told the reporter?
- What is the name of the reporter who covered the story?

Internet and Database Stories

- How long are the stories?
- Do they include interviews?
- Who appears to be quoted more often, and why?
- How long are their quotes, and what do you think of what they said?
- If you had been interviewed for the same story, what would you have told the reporter?
- What is the name of the reporter who covered the story?

Based on this information, you can apply your knowledge by:

- Knowing what kinds of stories they cover.
- Targeting the most appropriate news organization who will be interested in your story.
- Identifying the most appropriate reporter.
- Preparing the kinds of sound bites or ink bites they prefer.
- Providing the news organization with the best visual to help show your story.

Reading, watching, and listening to the news organizations offers one of the best and affordable continuing education you can obtain on what stories they like to cover and new trends and developments that may effect your own efforts to generate news coverage. By becoming a student of the media and applying what you learn, you can make your own efforts more productive and effective.

The Bottom Line

- You can learn the kinds of stories that news organization may be interested in receiving and covering by being a student of the media.
- The information you learn about their story preferences can help you publicize yourself or your real estate company.

How to Generate Publicity: Announce Awards to Agents

Real Estate People

Century 21 A.H. Realty announced its top Winter Haven associate awards for December. Rebecca Brown was recognized as top lister of the month. Shirley Smith was recognized as super seller for volume and top seller in number of units closed. Carol Pilkenton closed the big deal residential transaction and Alisha Dala was recognized as having the most exclusive buyer brokerage agreements.

The Ledger
Lakeland, Fla.
June 8, 2005

Advice and Insights: Real estate brokers often recognize agents for being top producers, super sellers, best deal closers, having the most listing agreements, etc.

Issuing news releases about these awards can be a win-win-win for the companies, their agents, and the media: the real estate firm can get some important publicity; the agents will receive recognition in the community for their expertise and achievements; and newspapers will have a nice story to include in their business or real estate sections.

But you don't need to receive an award from your company in order to make news. It's often the recognition you receive from colleagues in the real estate industry that can result in news—and headlines—about you. A case in point:

Jilane Fenner Named REALTOR of the Year

Jilane Fenner was named Paul Bunyan Board's REALTOR® of the Year for 2006. Fenner has been a member of Paul Bunyan Board of REALTORS® since 1993, originally joining through the former North Country Homes Real Estate, BH&G. She opened Cadillac's first Exit franchise, Exit Reality of Greater Cadillac, in 2001.

Cadillac News
Nov. 10, 2006
Cadillac, Mich.

Chapter 27

How to Take Advantage of the Challenges Facing News Organizations

Their Problems Are Your Opportunities

News organizations across the country have their own problems to contend with as they try to do the best job they can to report the news. This chapter examines 11 of those problems and suggests five ways to exploit those problems to ensure news coverage about you or your real estate company.

The challenges you face in convincing the media to do stories about you or your real estate company are matched only by the challenges editors and reporters face in gathering and reporting the news.

In order to produce their final products—whether it's a daily newspaper, nightly TV news program, or hourly radio news segment—editors, producers, and their staff must contend with a never-ending series of daily or continuing hurdles. According to journalists I've met, worked with and talked to (and based on my own experience), these problems include:

- Making decisions on which scheduled events or activities to cover, especially if they will be held at the same time.

- Weeding out the truly newsworthy press releases from the hundreds of apparently superfluous, irrelevant, or poorly written ones that cross their desks every week. (See Chapter 34)

- Ensuring that the stories they cover and people they interview are a true reflection of their community.

- Maintaining the right mix of local, national, or international news that will be of interest to their audiences.

- Fact-checking stories to ensure that there are no errors.

- Looking for the best available experts to interview, help explain, or provide perspective to technical or complex stories.

- Taking or locating pictures, graphs, charts, or other illustrations to help explain and show their stories. (See Chapter 12)

- Maintaining staff morale in the face of budget cutbacks, mergers, and acquisitions among news organizations, and the creeping influence of some advertising departments on the news judgments of editorial personnel.

- Finding and keeping good reporters and support staff.

- Providing enough time and resources so reporters can adequately research a story and be properly prepared to interview people for it.

- Ensuring that the work of their reporters, editors, and producers meets the criteria of good journalism.

Turn Their Lemons into Your Lemonade

How do you turn the media's lemons into your lemonade to ensure that, despite their problems and difficulties, you're able to convince news organizations to do the stories you want about you or your company?

By going the extra mile to help make their jobs—and their decision to do stories about you—as easy as possible.

Here's how:

1. Help them with their homework.
   Provide them with as much background information as you think is appropriate about your story, including news releases, fact sheets, or other stories that have been written about you or the topic.

2. Don't wait until it's too late.
   Give editors and reporters as much advance notice as possible about scheduled events such as a news conferences or news-making special events.

3. Show them the story.
   Find the best possible visuals that will help show your story as well as tell it (see Chapter 12), and be sure to tell the news organizations about your visuals when you first call.

4. Give them ideas.

   Call editors and reporters with story ideas that you think they may be interested in, even though those ideas may not result in news coverage about you. By showing you are a resource of information and ideas, they will be more receptive to your calls later when you pitch a story about yourself.

5. Provide good sound bites (See Chapter 22).

   Once you have the media's attention, take full advantage of the opportunity by providing them with the quotes they need to help tell their story to their audiences. The better your quotes, the more likely it is that they'll be used—and that the reporters will come back to you in the future for more interviews.

The Bottom Line

- News organizations have their own challenges and limitations as they try to report the news.

- By making it as easy as possible for new outlets to do stories about you or your real estate firm, you will increase the likelihood of generating the publicity you want.

How to Generate Publicity: Get Elected or Appointed to an Important Position

Carol Griffith, vice president of ERA Griffith in Brighton, has been elected president of the Livingston Association of Realtors for 2005. She is a licensed real estate agent and broker and a member of the Michigan Association of Realtors.

Ann Arbor News
Nov. 4, 2004
Ann Arbor, Mich.

Advice and Insights: One of the benefits of taking a leadership role in groups and organizations is—or should be—being recognized in the media for your efforts. Whether you are elected to the board or top position of your local or state REALTOR® association, be sure they issue a news releases about this important achievement, and that you include the news release on your Web site and in your other marketing materials.

The same holds true if you are elected to lead groups or organizations outside of the real estate community, as this example illustrates:

Pembroke Realtors Take Pond to Heart
Jack Conway and Company real estate agent Erin Sullivan was recently elected vice president of the Pembroke Watershed Association, an all volunteer group dedicated to improving the quality of Pembroke's many ponds.

Pembroke Mariner
June 28, 2006
Pembroke, Mass.

Part III

The Six Gateways to Publicity

Chapter 28

How to Do Newspaper and Magazine Interviews

Why All Media Interviews Are Not the Same

This chapter discusses how newspapers differ from other types of news organizations, and how agents and brokers should conduct themselves during interviews.

There's something about a printed newspaper, magazine, or newsletter story that's unlike any other type of news coverage.

- You can touch it.

- You can feel it.

- You can photocopy it and send it to your mother, father, friends, family, and clients.

- You can include a copy in your press kit and marketing materials.

- You can scan it and post it on your Web site.

Not only is print coverage tactile and versatile, copies of it can be seen by many more people than those who saw it when it was published. And depending where it was published, the text of the story may find its way into an online database library, where future generations of readers, researchers, reporters, and columnists may come across it.

Ironically, many television and radio stations use newspaper and magazine articles as "tip sheets" for their own story ideas and often quote or refer to those stories in their newscasts. Why? Because the stations' news staffs are often too small or too busy to report or research the same stories themselves. Print stories also differ from other forms of news coverage in several important ways, as outlined in the accompanying media comparison chart in this chapter.

More so than other news organizations, newspapers and magazines tend to deal with topics in greater depth and detail; it is not unusual for them to publish several thousand words, or run a series of articles over a period of days or months about a particular topic. These longer articles, of course, represent tremendous opportunities for experts to be interviewed, since most reporters (or their editors) don't like to rely on just one expert or authority for quotes, opinions, or perspectives in a lengthy article.

Convincing newspaper reporters to do a story about you is no different than trying to get other journalists to cover you (see Chapter 3). What is different, however, is when the reporter comes to your office or home to interview you for the article. Be sure to keep the following four points in mind:

1. Newspaper reporters can do more than simply report what you said. As trained observers, they can also convey to readers your demeanor and mannerisms during the interview, how you talked, how you dressed, and how you answered (or evaded) their questions. Just as you'd be on your best behavior for a television interview, realize that everything you say or do during a print interview could be mentioned or reported in the story.

2. Don't be lulled into a false sense of security or complacency. In an effort to help "loosen you up," the journalist may start the interview by talking about a completely different subject, and then slowly discuss the matter at hand. *Always keep in mind the three major points you want to make during the interview, and try not to let the reporter get you off track* (See Chapter 21).

3. Reporters can have roving eyes. If they will be coming to your home or office for the interview, make sure that you haven't left any important or embarrassing documents or other materials where the reporter can see them.

4. Don't assume that reporters can't read upside down, as happened to one of my PR clients. After an in-office interview with a reporter, the client was surprised to read in the next day's paper story excerpts from a confidential memo he had left on the corner of his desk that he assumed the reporter could not read. (For more advice on media interviews, see Chapters 20 and 21 and Part III.)

Media Comparison Chart

While it's impossible to categorize or describe every news organizations in the United States, it is possible to make some helpful basic comparisons and generalizations about them. The following charts describe and illustrate the differences among major types of news organizations in terms of frequency, deadlines, etc. For more detailed information, be sure to contact individual news organizations.

Frequency

Papers: Daily (although their online editions may be updated on an hourly basis with late-breaking news and headlines from their staff and wire services).

Magazines: Weekly, monthly, or quarterly.

Newsletters: Daily, weekly, monthly, or quarterly.

Wires: 24/7.

TV: Usually in the morning and evening.

Radio: Can be hourly.

Web sites: 24/7.

Deadlines

Papers: Usually the day before publication, but some magazine inserts may be printed as much as a week before the rest of the paper.

Magazines: Several days or several weeks before publication.

Newsletters: Depends on the individual publication.

Wires: No set deadlines.

TV: Late afternoon for evening newscasts; late evenings for morning shows.

Radio: Can be several minutes prior to the newscast.

Web sites: No set deadlines.

Length of Story

Papers: 300 to 1,500 words.

Magazines: 500 to 5,000 words.

Newsletters: 50 to 500 words.

Wires: 200 to 00 words.

TV: 90 seconds.

Radio: 10 to 60 seconds.

Web sites: 200 to 500 words.

Expertise of reporters in the stories they cover

Newspapers: Depends on the size and circulation of the paper. At larger dailies, many reporters will work the same beat for several months or years, and develop a greater knowledge of the stories than the people they interview for them.

Magazines:	Many magazines rely on freelance writers for stories, so their expertise can vary from naive to expert.
Newsletters:	Most are specialists.
Wires:	Many are specialists or have covered the beat for several months.
TV:	Most are general assignment reporters.
Radio:	Almost all are general assignment reporters.
Web sites:	Varies.

Best time to reach them

Newspapers:	Before lunch, when they first arrive for work. Never call a reporter late in the afternoon when he or she will most likely be finishing a story for the next day's paper. The exception to this rule is when a reporter calls you in the afternoon or evening. You should try to return their calls immediately.
Magazines:	Anytime.
Newsletters:	Regular business hours.
Wires:	Regular business hours.
TV:	Up until about an hour before their newscast.
Radio:	Up until about 10 minutes prior to their newscast.
Web sites:	Anytime via e-mail.

Corrections policies

Newspapers:	Usually prints corrections the day after the original story was published.
Magazines:	Weeks or months after the error was printed.
Newsletters:	Usually prints corrections in the next issue.
Wires:	Almost immediately after the mistake is called to their attention.
TV:	While most TV stations do not issue corrections, it's still important that you call as soon as you realize the mistake. Although the station might not issue a correction, they may correct the information for use in the next newscast.
Radio:	The next newscast, if you call as soon as you hear the mistake.
Web sites:	Usually makes corrections as soon as they are received.

Length of quotes they use in their stories

Newspapers:	5 to 50 words.
Magazines:	5 to 50 words.
Radio:	5 to 5 seconds.

| TV: | 7 seconds (and shrinking). |
| Web sites: | 5 to 50 words. |

Audiences

Newspapers:	General public.
Magazines:	Readers interested in the topics they cover.
Newsletter:	Subscribers interested in the topics they cover.
Wires:	General public.
Radio:	General public.
TV:	General public.
Web sites:	Visitors interested in the topics they cover.

Competition

Newspapers:	Most metropolitan areas have only one daily newspaper and several non-competing weekly papers that serve smaller communities or neighborhoods.
Magazines:	There are many competing publications on the national level, almost no competition among magazines locally.
Radio:	The larger the area, the more likely that they will have competing stations. In Southern California, for example, there are more than 100 radio stations.
Newsletters:	Depends on the topics they cover.
Wires:	There are five major wire services (AP, Reuters, Bloomberg, Dow Jones, and UPI).
TV:	Very competitive, with most areas having between two and five stations.
Web sites:	Millions.

The Bottom Line

- Television and radio stations often use newspapers as cheat sheets for story ideas.

- Know the differences between different kinds of media outlets so you can customize your publicity efforts accordingly.

How to Generate Publicity: Promote Your Talents

Real estate broker Steven Shoen, of Shoen Real Estate in Novato, has released a CD of his original songs called "On Top of the World." About 40 percent of the proceeds of the CD, produced by Jefferson Starship's Pete Sears, will benefit Marin Children's Garden. Shoen, a volunteer performer for Bread and Roses in Corte Madera, has been a Marin real estate broker for more than 20 years. For information on the CD, call 382-1600.

Marin Independent Journal
April 25, 2004
San Rafael, Calif.

Advice and Insights: Agents and brokers often have talents that have nothing to do with listing or selling property but which can make them newsworthy just the same.

Savvy real estate professionals will not be shy in converting their talents into news hooks and story angles that can help attract the interest of the media. And the more you can build into the story—such as Shoen's decision to donate a portion of the proceeds of his CD or referring to his association with well-known bands—the better the story will be.

Chapter 29

How to Do Television Interviews

The Camera Is Always on

This chapter includes advice on how to do interviews on television news shows and features a list of 12 things real estate agents should do to get the most out of their interviews.

Television interviews provide a great opportunity for you to become known by a large number of people in a very short period of time. In fact, surveys show that more people get their news from television than from any other source.

So if you think there is a lot riding on your interview with a TV reporter, you're absolutely right. That's because even though you have an important message or story to talk about, what the public thinks of your message and whether they believe what you say is often determined by how you dress, how you talk, what you say, and how you say it on television.

Here are some tips to help you get the most out of your TV interviews:

- If you will be interviewed in a studio, arrive early so you can meet the production staff, take a look at the set, make sure you are comfortable in the chair you'll be sitting in, etc.

- Know the three most important points you want to make during the interview, and find ways to return to those points throughout the interview.

- Look at the reporter during the interview, not at the camera.

- Don't fidget, twitch in your chair, or do anything that will detract viewers from your message.

- Do not wear large or distracting jewelry.

- Glance in a mirror before the interview to make sure you look the way you want.

- Use appropriate gestures to help make or emphasize your points.

- Be positive, upbeat and confident in your answers, manner and demeanor.

- Smile and keep a pleasant expression on your face at all times.

- Keep your answers short, usually 20 to 30 seconds.

- Avoid speaking in a monotone or speaking too fast; vary your voice pitch and tone to help make or emphasize your points and message.

- Bring or refer the reporter to any visuals that will help show your story or make your point.

Barry Crotty is a REALTOR® with Coldwell Banker in Greenbrae Calif. who has been interviewed several times on television. He notes that, "You must be real clear what you want to communicate to the television reporter. You should have three main points you want to get across, and not get sidetracked with their questions. The more prepared you are, the more comfortable you will be when you are interviewed."

David Stempler, president of the Air Travelers Association, has been interviewed hundreds of times by the media. He recalls that, "I was nervous about getting things right the first few times I did TV interviews. But I realized that if what I did was successful, then there would be many more interviews in the future. And if I didn't get it right the first time, then I'd get it right the next time. That realization helped me to relax and not to be so worried about getting every word right or making a minor flub.

"Reporters have told me that they don't mind minor mistakes because it makes you look more like a regular person, not a staged professional. Today, if I'm doing a taped TV or radio interview and do make a mistake, I can always tell the reporter that I wasn't happy with my answer, and ask to do it over again."

How to Dress for TV Interviews

Medialink Inc., a news video production company, offers the following advice on how to dress for television interviews:

Dress the Way You Want Your Peers to See You

- Blues and grays always work best, giving an aura of professionalism.

- Avoid herringbone and other patterns in suits because they can cause electronic confusion for the camera.

- A simple stripe or muted design is acceptable but solids work best. Women should wear a jacket or a blouse with buttons to allow for a lavaliere microphone. Never wear black or white clothing on camera.

The Natural Look Always Applies

- If you wear glasses, wear glasses on-camera. Chrome or metal frames sometimes cause problems, as do certain lenses.
- Angle your glasses down slightly and try to use simple frames like light tortoiseshell.

Avoid Elaborate Jewelry

- Avoid fancy bracelets and necklaces since they may cause flash or noise interference with microphones. A tailored look is preferable.

Simple Makeup

- Makeup is vital for any on-camera appearance. Medialink's experts recommend keeping it simple and making sure the makeup is well blended.
- Be certain to check your entire look before a recorded interview and make certain your makeup is retouched if there are a number of "takes."

Don't Wear New Clothes

- You should be comfortable in your outfit, so don't wear anything new to an on-camera appearance.
- Check the mirror prior to the interview to make sure you are pleased with your appearance.
- If your appearance requires you to sit, be certain you have checked your appearance in the mirror in that same position.

Of course, all the advice in the world won't be of any help unless you practice using it.

- One way to practice is to stand in front of a mirror and pretend you're being interviewed on TV.
- A step up from that is to use a video camera to tape your practice interviews.
- Finally, you may want to invest the time and money to retain the services of a professional media trainer who can provide important feedback to your mock interviews and provide expert advice on how to craft your message, deliver sound bites, answer a reporter's questions, etc.

For additional advice on interviews, see Chapters 20 and 21 and Part III.

The Bottom Line

- Too much will be riding on the outcome of your television interview not to prepare as much as possible beforehand.
- What you wear and your body language are just as important as what you say.

How to Generate Publicity: Launch a New Web Site

Realtor Renee Adelmann has announced a new Web site called Eichlerforsale. com, designed to showcase "California modern" homes and condominiums built by Joseph Eichler. Adelmann is a Realtor with Keller William Realty.

Marin Independent Journal
April 26, 2006
San Rafael, Calif.

Advice and Insights: Given the current number of real estate-related Web sites, why in the world would any news organization publish a story about a new site going online? Because the site offered news or information about a particular real estate topic that cannot be found anywhere else, that's why. But the above story was not a fluke.

To get publicity for your company's Web site, sometimes all you have to do is add more bells and whistles to it:

The Real-Estate-Broker Wars: With Home Sales Slowing, Old-Line and Discount Firms Tout Range of New Services
A number of full-service Realtors are adding tools that allow sellers to better track buyer interest and other activity. Real Living, Inc., a regional brokerage firm based in Columbus, Ohio, recently beefed up its Web site to enable sellers to see how many people have looked at their homes and what comments they made.

The Wall Street Journal
May 23, 2006

Chapter 30

How to Do Radio News Interviews

Your Voice Is Your Business Card

This chapter discusses the best ways to act during live or taped radio interviews. Also includes a helpful checklist of nine things real estate agents should do before, during and after interviews.

The nice thing about radio interviews is that no one cares how you look or dress. And there is absolutely no need to get nervous about it—even though your image and reputation is riding on every word you say and how you say it (gulp!).

But seriously, radio interviews can be one of the easiest types of interviews to do for most people. That's because:

- Since most news stories are relatively short (often in the 30 to 40 second range), your sound bite will be relatively short as well.

- Almost all radio interviews are done by phone, so you can talk to the reporter from the comfort of your home, or even on a cell phone in a parked car.

- You can have as much background information you need in front of you during the interview and you can refer to it as often as you need to.

- Most radio interviews are taped, so if you don't like an answer you gave or flubbed a response, simply tell the reporter that you want to give your answer over again.

Here's what you can do to help guarantee your radio interviews go as smoothly as possible:

- Make sure there are no distractions in the room where you will call from, and that there are no street noises, barking dogs, etc. that will be picked up by the phone.

- Jot down on a legal pad the three major points you want to cover during the interview and check them off as you make them during the interview.

- Speak in a conversational tone.

- Stand up when you speak (your voice will be stronger and deeper than when sitting down).

- Smile when you talk (it helps make you sound more pleasant, relaxed and energetic).

- Practice what you want to say ahead of time so your answers don't run more than 10 to 15 seconds.

- Organize any reference materials you may need during the interview so you won't have to shuffle through papers to find the information you need.

- Find out from the reporter whether you are to call her or if she is to call you.

- Make sure you have a phone number where you can reach the reporter before the interview. If the reporter will call you for the interview, be sure to keep your line clear as much as possible prior to the time of the interview.

Finally, use a tape recorder to practice delivering your answers; ask a friend, family member, or colleague to "play reporter" and ask you a combination of easy and difficult questions.

Make arrangements beforehand to tape record your radio interview, and then go back to see hear how you did. What would you like to do differently or better the next time?

See Chapters 20 and 21 and Part III for more advice on conducting interviews.

The Bottom Line

- Radio interviews can be one of the easiest types of interviews to do for most real estate agents and brokers.

- Prepare and practice what you want to say prior to the interview.

- Tape your interview or obtain a copy afterwards so you can critique your performance.

How to Generate Publicity: Seek Help From A Higher Power

Some Say Key to Selling Home Is Statue, Prayer
San Antonio Realtor Mark Wood took a good look at the house he was about to list, let out a big sigh, and thought, "This is going to be hard to sell." The house was in a not-great location, and it had quirky upgrades that would probably not appeal to prospective buyers. Instead of running to Home Depot for quick makeover ideas, Wood decided to turn to a higher power, St. Joseph, the patron saint of home seekers. Wood was skeptical about St. Joseph's power to sell a house, but he was also desperate. "I'm not Catholic, but I thought, 'What could it hurt?'" he said.

San Antonio Express News
Oct. 14, 2006
San Antonio, Texas

Advice and Insights: In a changing real estate market, agents are often forced to go the extra mile to promote their listings—and themselves. It's what you do that goes above the call of duty to help sell a property that can also grab the attention of the local media.

Chapter 31

How to Be a Great Guest on a Radio Talk Show

Can You Hear Me? Am I on the Air?

How you should conduct yourself when you go on the radio.

Radio talk shows are important and influential forums for real estate agents and brokers to be heard by millions of interested, curious, and oftentimes opinionated listeners.

The number of these radio programs has proliferated in recent years, thanks to the large ratings some of the more popular hosts are able to generate for stations, and the fact that several all-music stations across the country have converted to all-talk formats. As the programs have grown in number, they have also grown in influence, with hosts sometimes egging listeners on to urge their lawmakers to pass or defeat legislation.

For all the popularity and impact these shows have, these programs can be a good place for you to share your knowledge, expertise, and perspectives on real estate.

- Topics and guests are usually decided solely by the host or his producer. Unlike a newspaper where there can be scores of reporters to whom you can pitch your story idea, if you strike out with the host or producer, there is no one else to turn to.

- You must know your topic inside and out. Although you can bring background or reference material with you to the studio or keep it in front of you at home, you may have no chance to use it. Most shows are done live and you won't have an opportunity to "look something up" while millions of people wait for your answer.

- Listen to the show several times beforehand to get a feel for the topics and issues they discuss, the interviewing style of the host, and the kinds of questions callers ask of guests.

- You should have a strong, clear speaking voice that conveys confidence and authority to the listening audience.

- While it's important that you prepare for the show as you would for any other type of interview, radio call-in hosts may be less willing to share with you the list of questions they'll ask you. That's because they want their guests to be and sound as spontaneous as possible.

- You should be able to perform well under pressure. A lot will be riding on your ability to explain yourself and answer questions in front of a live audience.

How to Generate Publicity: Hold a Blood Drive

Realtors Taking a Challenge to Heart
Aldridge and Southerland real estate agency took an open challenge from Prudential Prime Properties to heart—literally. In November, employees from Prudential donated more than 20 units of blood, giving the American Red Cross donation center on Cromwell Drive its best day since moving to the new facility last year.

Daily Reflector
Jan. 21, 2005
Greenville N.C.

Advice and Insights: Giving blood or holding blood drives are hardly new ideas. But when real estate companies get involved, or challenge each other to give blood, then you have the makings of a news story.

Chapter 32

Why Newswire Services Can Be Important for You

Sudden Impact

Newswires provide reports and feature stories to thousands of television stations, radio stations, newspapers, and magazines; they are the fastest and most effective ways for people to tell their stories to the world.

News organizations receive leads and ideas for stories from several different sources, including their own reporters, current events, viewers, readers, listeners, PR firms, and individuals and companies seeking news coverage about their own activities and accomplishments.

Ironically, an important source of story ideas for news organizations is other news organizations: the Associated Press, Dow Jones, Reuters, Bloomberg News, United Press International, and other wire services that distribute news and information to subscribers 24 hours a day, seven days a week.

Thousands of major TV stations, radio stations, newspapers, and magazines around the world depend on these services for a steady stream of news reports and feature stories they can use in newscasts or publications, or as the basis from which their reporters can prepare their own stories. Even some Web sites and Internet services, such as America Online, provide visitors and users with excerpts from or full-text versions of selected wire service copy for their own information or entertainment.

They all have a common problem, however, in trying to determine what information is relevant for their audiences as their editors and writers sift through the hundreds of news releases they receive every day.

Newswire services can be the fastest and most effective way to tell your story to the world, or to help convince other news organizations that their story is worth reporting to others.

Unfortunately, the larger the news organization, the bigger the hurdles you'll face in convincing them to do a story about you, and answering the questions of who cares and why (see Chapter 3).

News services are no different. You must be able to convince a wire service editor or reporter why your story will be of interest to their subscribers, and why what you have to say will be interesting to their readers, viewers, or listeners.

Of course, some newswire services are easier to convince to do stories about you than others are. For three of them (PR Newswire, BusinessWire, and US Newswire), all you need is money and a well-written news release on the letterhead of your corporation or organization.

At a meeting of the Los Angeles chapter of the Public Relations Society of America, officials of the Associated Press, United Press International, Reuters, and City News Service provided several suggestions for placing stories on their wires and with other news organizations. As reported by *Jack O'Dwyer's Newsletter*, their recommendations included:

- Do not send multiple copies of your release to the same person or even to several different people at one location.
- Use the "who, what, when, where" format to describe the event.
- Its okay to pitch the event via phone but don't call to ask if a fax has been received.
- Don't use e-mail to pitch an idea.
- Fax releases by noon so reporters have time to call back later in the day with questions.
- Make sure the release is complete, with evening and weekend contact numbers as well as cell phone numbers.
- When pitching a bureau, contact the one in the city where your company is based.
- Feel free to approach business editors with a list of experts who they can contact for comment on stories.

The Bottom Line

- News organizations get story leads and ideas from a variety of sources.
- Each news organization must decide what news is relevant to their audience.
- Newswires can be an effective way to tell your story to the greatest number of people.

How to Generate Publicity: Turn Lemons into Lemonade

Real Estate Spoken Here
When Cristina Matos became a real estate agent three years ago, she worried that her accent, a reminder of her Portuguese origins, would scare off potential clients. "I was absolutely wrong," declares the Corcoran Group sales agent. Indeed, her knowledge of Portuguese and Spanish has been a great professional asset, Matos says. Of the 10 sales she says she has made so far this year in Southampton, only one of the buyers was a native English speaker, and most were referrals from other Spanish or Portuguese speakers.

As new waves of workers from all over the world enter Long Island's housing markets, multilingual real estate agents such as Matos are finding themselves in increasing demand, and real estate companies are scrambling to show their international colors.

Newsday
Nov. 9, 2006
Melville, New York

Advice and Insights: As this story illustrates, the skills or talents you bring to the real estate profession can be interesting and newsworthy to journalists. Don't be complacent, self-deprecating, or shy about your abilities since one of your competitors who has a particular ability—and is not reluctant to tell the media about it—may beat you to the punch.

Chapter 33

How to Use the Internet as a Publicity Tool

The New Level Playing Field

This chapter looks at the benefits and advantages of Web sites as part of your publicity efforts, and discusses four things you can do to help ensure reporters can find you on the Internet.

The Internet is one of the most powerful tools real estate agents and brokers can use to tell their stories to potential clients, not to mention reporters who regard the Web as an important source of information and story ideas.

Many news organizations regard the Internet as a source of information and story ideas. Indeed, Web sites have become the ultimate "level playing field" where everyone (including real estate agents and brokers) has an equal chance to tell their stories to the world.

Among the millions of organizations that have established their own Web sites are thousands of newspapers and television and radio stations. Seeking to escape the constraints of printing their editions once a day or broadcasting their news on a set schedule, these news outlets use the Internet to distribute their news and other content 24/7.

You can take advantage of this level playing field by sending appropriate Web sites copies of your news release or other press materials. And blogs and podcasts provide real estate professionals with opportunities to post their observations and opinions on their own or other Web sites.

Since even basic Web sites are now easy and affordable to produce and maintain, you should also launch your own site to promote yourself and ensure that reporters and editors can read all about you or your company any time they want.

- By establishing your own blogs and podcasts on your site, you'll have two additional ways to quickly post information, announcements, and other information.
- Update your blogs and podcasts on a frequent basis to give people a reason to return to them often.

Be sure to make it as easy as possible for the media to find the information they need on your site. That means setting up a "press room" or "news" section on your home page, and linking it your news releases, fact sheets, news clippings, and other press materials.

To make it as easy as possible for journalists to find your Web site:

1. Be sure your site and key identifying words are listed with the major Internet search engines.

2. Include your Web site address on all materials that you send to the media, including news releases, press kits, news advisories, and business cards.

3. Issue a news release via PR Newswire or BusinessWire, announcing your Web site to the media, and describe your areas of expertise for media interviews.

4. Mention your Web site address during answering machine or voice-mail greetings.

But before you tell the world about your Web site, make sure you've made it the best it can possibly be. That means hiring an experienced Web site designer to prepare your site and reading up on the latest advice for "best of class" Web sites, making note of Web sites that you like.

Finally, since there are so many real estate Web sites already up and running, it is important that you take steps to make your site interesting or unique to help it stand out from all the others and give news organizations a reason to do stories about it.

If your site attracts a lot of visitors, then its popularity might be newsworthy. That's exactly what happened to this real estate company:

Coldwell's main local site, floridamoves. com, snagged nearly 6 million visitors last year. In addition to detailed property information, the site features automatic e-mail notification when a buyer's search criteria match a specific property description.

Sarasota Herald-Tribune
July 31, 2006
Sarasota, Fla.

The Bottom Line

- The Internet provides a level playing field for real estate agents and brokers to tell their stories to the media.
- Be sure to include your Web site address on all of your press materials.
- Include a "press room" on your site so reporters will know where to go for information about your company, activities, or accomplishments.

How to Generate Publicity: Make a Speech

Incentives, Price Cuts Power House Sales
At the Oct. 19 Northern Virginia Association of Realtors Convention and Trade Show, a presentation delivered by broker David Howell of McEnearney Associates in McLean showed that more than half of all properties going under contract in Northern Virginia in September had a price reduction from the original asking price.

Washington Times
Nov. 10, 2006
Washington, DC

Advice and Insights: For the thousands of people who are invited each year to make remarks or presentations to conventions, workshops, or other meetings, public speaking represents an important opportunity to help spread the word about their own accomplishments, activities, opinions, or expertise.

Speeches are also an excellent way to position yourself as an expert on any number of real estate-related topics or issues, and to help attract the interest of editors, reporters, and columnists to interview you for stories in which you have some expertise. (For advice on making speeches, see Chapter 17.)

Of course, depending on your local housing market, what you have to say may be more positive and upbeat than in other parts of the country. And don't limit your public speeches to colleagues—branch out and offer to speak to local chambers of commerce, service organizations, etc. as this broker did:

Broker: County Housing Market Still Strong
The local real estate market has been strong the past few years and Roseburg real estate broker Neil Hummel said he doesn't see any reason for that to change anytime soon. Speaking Monday at the Noon Forum sponsored by the Roseburg Area Chamber of Commerce, Hummell said home values increased last year by 23 percent. That bettered the previous year's gain by nine points. "There isn't anything that I've seen like that in my career," he said.

The News Review
April 4, 2006
Winchester, Ore.

Every speech has the potential to result in news coverage about your remarks before two audiences: those who read about it before your presentation, and those who read about it afterwards. Here are six steps you can take to make sure you take full advantage of every speaking opportunity that comes your way:

1. Before your speech, send a news release announcing your appearance to the editors of appropriate newsletters, magazines, newspapers, or other news outlets.

2. Ask the people who invited you to speak to place a story about your upcoming presentation in their organization's newsletter, e-mail messages to their members, and on their Web site.

3. If you will be speaking at a convention or conference where there is a press-room for the reporters who are covering the event, drop off copies of your release at the room when you arrive at the site. If time permits, introduce yourself to any reporters in the room, tell them about your speech, and offer to be available for interviews if they are interested in doing a story about it.

4. If appropriate, record your speech and post copies of it on your Web site, in a podcast, or post excerpts from your remarks in a blog.

5. Immediately after your appearance, prepare and distribute a news release about your speech, who you spoke to, highlights from your remarks, etc.

6. Your clients or prospects may be as interested in what you have to say as reporters, so consider sending copies of the news release or the text of your remarks to your marketing lists.

Part IV

How to Use Key PR Tools

So That's How They Do It!

An explanation of 15 effective techniques, tactics, and tools of the trade real estate agents can use immediately to help generate publicity.

Chapter 34

News Releases

A Storyteller's Best Friend

Ten secrets for preparing news releases that can help convince reporters to do stories about you or your real estate company.

The news release represents the cornerstone of the efforts of many real estate agents and brokers to generate news coverage about themselves. Indeed, the news release is perhaps the most important and effective way to tell the media and the world who you are, what you are doing, why you are doing it, when you are doing it, and how you are doing it.

These one- to two-page documents should:

- Answer the all-important question of "who cares and why?" (See Chapter 3)
- Include the who, what, when, where, why, and how of your story (whether it's an announcement about the hiring of new agents, the opening of a new office, or an important award or recognition your company has received).

Sometimes, news organizations will include the fact that you issued a news release in the story that the news release helps create. For example:

Two Albany Real Estate Firms Merge
GD Michelson Real Estate in Albany, N.Y., has merged with the larger Albany Realty Group LLC, the principals announced Friday. Gerry and Diana Michelson and four of their agents—Herb Cohen, Bill Kellert, Nancy Rezek and Jessica Balkis—transferred their real estate licenses to Albany Realty Group in July. The Michelsons have served the Albany region for 30 years, with experience

in construction, commercial and residential real estate, *according to a press release.* (Italics added for emphasis).

The Business Review
July 31, 2006
Albany, New York

Corporate America spends a lot of time, money, and effort on preparing and distributing news releases. Writing in *PRWeek,* Katherine Spellissy, vice president of client services at Ink, Inc., estimated the tab might be as high as $1 billion *every year.* Unfortunately, most of that money appears to be wasted. The magazine surveyed key editors and reporters who said that as many as 99 percent of the materials they receive are trashed because the releases are irrelevant to their needs, void of any real news, or poorly written.

The Recipe for an Effective News Release

The best news releases become self-fulfilling prophecies: the more they *read* like real news stories and are sent to reporters who will be interested in receiving them, the more likely it is that they will *become* news stories.

Unfortunately, there is no such thing as a one-size-fits-all, fill-in-the-blanks news release. Rather, you should think of your news release as a custom-made dress or suit which must be carefully tailored to tell your own story in the most effective and attention-getting way possible. You can customize your news release in the following ways (examples are from a news release I wrote for the Marin Association of REALTORS® are included in italics) and use the template in this chapter to help prepare your own customized news release.

1. Include your name, daytime, and evening phone numbers, and e-mail and Web site addresses at the top of the first page if reporters have questions about the release or want to interview you.

2. If appropriate, place your announcement in the context of relevant trends or developments.

3. Organize the information in the release as if it were a pyramid, with the most critical information at the top and the least important at the bottom.

4. Summarize the announcement with an attention-getting headline.
    Marin REALTORS® Call for Passage of Proposed Second Unit Amnesty Program

5. Write a succinct opening paragraph that summarizes your story or announcement.

The Marin Association of REALTORS® today called on the county board of supervisors to pass a proposed building permit amnesty program for homeowners who live in the unincorporated areas of Marin County.

6. Explain the impact your story or announcement will have on audiences of the news organizations that receive the release.

   MAR CEO Edward Segal told the board that the measure "can help ensure that second units meet basic health and safety guidelines, has the potential to provide needed affordable housing, can make properties more marketable for homeowners, and provide peace-of-mind to prospective home buyers."

7. If appropriate, include a call for action.

   Segal said he hopes passage of the ordinance "will be the first step towards implementing a building permit amnesty program for all homeowners. What make sense for a small group of second unit owners, also makes sense for other homeowners in unincorporated areas of the county who did not obtain the necessary building permits for their construction or home improvement projects. If these other homeowners can prove that their work is up to code, then they are as deserving of a clean slate as the owners of second units," he said.

8. Include appropriate facts, figures, and background information.

   According to Novato officials, more than 850 people participated in the city's two amnesty programs, which were conducted between 1998 and 2000. The city collected more than $160,000 in fees and evaluated more than $3 million worth of work.

   In 2003, MAR launched a year-round public service campaign to educate the public about the criteria for obtaining building permits in their communities, and extended an offer to all local governments to help promote and publicize their amnesty programs to the public and the real estate community. The association maintains a building permit information center on its Web site at www.MarinCountyRealtors.com.

9. If appropriate, include a picture that illustrates the announcement, accompanied by a descriptive caption (also called a cut line).

10. To signify the end of the release, insert -30- at the end of the bottom on the last page of the release and center it on the page.

News Release Template

For Immediate Release
Tuesday, Nov. 16, 2006

Media Contact:
Edward Segal, CEO
Marin Association of REALTORS®
415-507-1011
Edwards@marincountyrealtors.com

Marin REALTORS® Call for Passage of Proposed Second Unit Amnesty Program

(SAN RAFAEL)—The Marin Association of REALTORS® today called on the county board of supervisors to pass a proposed building permit amnesty program for homeowners who live in the unincorporated areas of Marin County.

MAR CEO Edward Segal told the board the measure "can help ensure that second units meet basic health and safety guidelines, has the potential to provide needed affordable housing, can make properties more marketable for homeowners, and provide peace-of-mind to prospective home buyers."

Segal said passage of the ordinance "should be the first step towards implementing a building permit amnesty program for all homeowners.

"What make sense for a small group second unit owners, also makes sense for other homeowners in unincorporated areas of the county who did not obtain the necessary building permits for their construction or home improvement projects. If these other homeowners can prove that their work is up to code, then they are as deserving of a clean slate as the owners of second units," he said.

According to Novato officials, more than 850 people participated in the city's two amnesty programs, which were conducted between 1998 and 2000. The city collected more than $160,000 in fees and evaluated more than $3 million worth of work.

In 2003, MAR launched a year-round public service campaign to educate the public about the criteria for obtaining building permits in their communities, and extended an offer to all local governments to help promote and publicize their amnesty programs to the public and the real estate community. The 1,700 member association maintains a building permit information center on its Web site at www.MarinCountyRealtors.com.

- 30 -

Ensure Your Success

While it's impossible to predict how many stories your news release generates, there are several steps you can take to ensure that your efforts are successful:

- In addition to writing your releases as if they were newspaper stories, be sure to abide by the same rules for grammar and punctuation that reporters follow when they write their articles. Or refer to the *Associated Press Stylebook* which can be found at most libraries and bookstores.

- Send the news release to news organizations that will be most interested in receiving it. If you have any doubts, call editors, reporters, and columnists in advance and ask if they are interested in the subject of the release.

- Make sure the list of reporters receiving the release is current and accurate.

- If possible, send the news release to reporters on traditionally slow news days, such as Mondays or Saturdays, and send it earlier in the day rather than later. (See Chapter 18)

- Try to send your releases between 10 AM to Noon, since that's when most editors or reporters decide which stories they will do that day.

- Return calls from the media as soon as possible.

- Be prepared to answer any questions reporters may have about the information in the release.

If reporters are interested in doing a story based on the news release, they may call you for an interview or to ask for clarification or more information. Then again, they may not call at all, and write their stories based on the information you've included in the release.

While it is certainly not standard practice, if the release is well-written and meets the criteria of a legitimate news story, sometimes a news organization will simply run the release—or use major excerpts from it—almost exactly as you gave it to them. Now that's my idea of good journalism!

For the latest examples of news releases, click on the "tools of the trade" link on the home page of www.ProfitByPublicity.com. Also, be sure to visit my blog at http://ProfitByPublicity.blogspot.com.

The Bottom Line

- News releases are the most important tool you can use to help generate news coverage about you or your real estate company.

- There is no such thing as a one-size-fits-all news release—each must be written and customized for the story they seek to promote.
- The more your releases read *as if* they are news stories, the more likely it is that they will *become* news stories.

How to Generate Publicity: Discuss Local Real Estate Trends

The Blossoming of Canyon Lake

Area real estate agents say the rapid growth and appreciation [in Canyon Lake] have been the result of a kind of perfect storm in real estate: developers eager to cash in on the high-dollar hunger for lake views; out-of-state investors cashing out of waning markets on the East and West coasts and desperate to find a place to park their money to avoid capital gains taxes; and San Antonio families willing to commute to find affordable housing in the area. [New] subdivisions are attracting plenty of non-Texas interest. "We are seeing people from California, Florida, Colorado," said Ed Mullins, a Canyon Lake real estate agent with Mickey Ferrell Realtors. "I even had someone in from Turkey." According to local real estate agents, as the housing market worsens around the country, especially in Florida and California, people are trying to get out while they can and reinvest their money is real estate markets that are still appreciating such as Texas.

San Antonio Express
Nov. 4, 2006
San Antonio, Texas

Advice and Insights: To paraphrase Tip O'Neill, the late Speaker of the House of Representatives, "All real estate is local." Even though a housing market in one part of the country may be cooling off, it could be heating up somewhere else. If your market is different from others in some way—such as prices, inventory, demographics, etc—call the anomaly to the attention of the press and position yourself as an expert who can discuss the matter.

Chapter 35

Fact Sheets

Stick with the Basics

Six tips for writing fact sheets that will attract the interest and meet the needs of the media.

Fact sheets are used to describe essential, complex, or background information reporters or columnists may need in order to fully understand or accurately report an event or news announcement. It may include information that is too long or complex to put into a news release.

Effective Fact Sheets

There are several steps you can take to help ensure that a fact sheet about your project or announcement will help editors and reporters to cover your story.

1. If the fact sheet will accompany a news release or press kit, only include background information that is too long or complex to put in a news release.

2. If the fact sheet will not accompany a news release, be sure the information you include is complete and self-explanatory.

3. Cite the source of all information, studies, or research.

4. Limit the length of the fact sheet to two single-spaced pages. The shorter the better.

5. Make the information visually appealing by using boldface headlines, informative sub-heads, and short paragraphs.

6. Include the name, phone number, e-mail, and Web site for reporters to contact if they have questions about any information in the fact sheet.

For the latest examples of fact sheets, click on the "tools of the trade" link on the home page of www.ProfitByPublicity.com. Also, be sure to visit my blog at http://ProfitByPublicity.blogspot.com.

The Bottom Line

- Fact sheets provide essential information journalists need to understand or report a story.

How to Generate Publicity: Go Where the People Are

Real Estate Firm Opens First Kiosk at Mall
Next week, Holliston resident Mary Condon, formerly of Keller Williams Westborough, will open People's Choice Real Estate, "a fully functional, on-line, interactive and manned real estate office" located in the Natick Mall. Condon, who is seeking to have 45 agents working with her at the kiosk office, is preparing to have five laptop computers, a wide-screen, 22-inch monitor, a printer, scanner, copier, appropriate software for the real estate market, speakers and displays. The whole set up, including rental fees, will cost a pretty penny, she said, but it's not about the money.

The agents will show passersby or potential buyers and sellers how they can get the best from the Realtor Web sites and, "of course, we will list your home now and become your buyer agent now," she said. The beauty of being in the mall, she said, is being available just at the moment someone comes up with a real estate question.

Daily News Transcript
Nov. 24, 2006
Dedham, Mass.

Advice and Insights: You've heard how important it can be to think outside the box? This story shows the importance of marketing outside your brick and mortar office. Indeed, your local newspaper or TV station may be as interested in *where* you market yourself as they are in the unique or unusual ways in *how* you market your services and expertise.

Chapter 36

Press Kits

Everything Reporters Need to Know about You

Nineteen do's and don'ts for preparing effective press kits about you or your company.

In telling your story to the media, neatness and organization counts.

Reporters and columnists receive hundreds of e-mails, letters, and packages every week from people, companies, or organizations seeking publicity. They simply do not have the time, inclination, or patience to wade through all the material in their inbox to find those few nuggets of news that will lead them to do interviews or prepare stories.

To help overcome this hurdle, prepare and tell your story in an organized and systematic way that will make it as easy as possible for the reporter to determine the newsworthiness of you or your real estate company.

A well-prepared press kit, whether printed or posted on your Web site, will do just that.

Online press kits are the easiest and most effective to produce since they can be posted to your Web site quickly and updated as needed. Most online press kits include:

- Company profile.
- Biographical information.
- Head and shoulder photos of corporate officers.
- Fact sheet about the company, agent, or event.
- If appropriate, a list of clients.
- Link to archive of past news releases.

- Link to archive of past news coverage.
- Contact information so editors and reporters can reach you.

A printed press kit, usually in the form of a standard two-pocket folder, is a complete package of information that provides reporters with everything they need to know about your story or news announcement.

Checklist

While each press kit must be prepared and customized to explain the story or announcement in the most effective way possible, many kits contain the following components in this order:

- Cover memo or letter with contact information.
- News release.
- Photo and cut line.
- Fact sheet.
- Biographical profile (if appropriate).
- Copies of related news clips.
- Copies of appropriate additional background information, such as news releases, newsletters, an annual report, or a relevant article that you wrote.

One of the most important ingredients of any press kit, however, is a heavy dose of common sense. Don't:

- Stuff the folder with useless or irrelevant information.
- Try to put so much material in the kit that the covers will not close.
- Jam the kit into an envelope that is so "skin tight" that it's impossible to open without damaging the kit.
- Spend a lot of money on designing or producing the kit or its contents.

While it is important for the finished product to look businesslike and professional, reporters will be more interested in being able to find and understand your story quickly, and less interested in looking at fancy or expensive graphics, pictures, or logos that get in the way of finding that story.

For the latest examples of online press kits, click on the "tools of the trade" link on the home page of www.ProfitByPublicity.com. Also, be sure to visit my blog at http://ProfitByPublicity.blogspot.com.

The Bottom Line

- Reporters don't have the time or patience to wade through all the materials and information they receive.
- Press kits can help journalists understand the news value of you or your real estate company.
- Online press kits are easy to produce and update, and have none of the overhead costs associated with printed version.

How to Generate Publicity: Announce the Hiring of New Agents

Alexander Joins Bosshardt Realty
Bosshardt Realty announced that Theresa Alexandra, Realtor, has joined the firm as a specialist in residential and new home sales. Prior to her real estate career, Theresa, a Florida Notary Republic, held management positions in accounting and bookkeeping for more than 10 years.

The Herald
April 9, 2006
Bradenton, Fla.

Advice and Insights: One of the most common sources of story angles for any size real estate company can be to announce the agents who have recently joined the firm.

While these stories are not likely to make it onto the front page of your local paper, they often will show up in its business section or be placed with other brief announcements in a digest or movers and shakers column. Don't expect long or in-depth stories, however. The most you can realistically hope for is a few lines of copy. But then, a little publicity is better than none at all.

Chapter 37

News Advisories

A Special Invitation

This chapter outlines the nine ingredients of news advisories that can help get reporters interested in doing stories about the events or activities of your real estate company.

News advisories are used to invite editors and reporters to attend a planned event, activity, or scheduled announcement, such as the grand opening of a new real estate office. They are best sent several days before the event and then once again so they are received a day before the event is held.

Effective News Advisories

There are several steps you can take to help ensure that news advisories about your project will result in media coverage. These steps, along with excerpts from a news advisory I wrote for the Marin Association of REALTORS®, follow:

1. Summarize your announcement with an attention-getting headline.
   Real Estate Agents Take Steps to Improve the Safety and Security of the Homes They Sell

2. Write a succinct opening paragraph that captures the who, what, when, where, why and, how of your announcement.
   This week more than 1,500 real estate agents in Marin County are taking steps to improve the safety and security of the thousands of homes they show to clients each year as the agents trade in their old electronic lock box keys for "state of the art" high tech infrared "smart keys."

3. Highlight and explain the most interesting or newsworthy aspects of your project. Keep the copy focused and factual.

The new technology represents a quantum leap over the 1955 introduction of the first mechanical lockbox device, which consisted of a Yale® bicycle lock with a sand-casted key container. By contrast, the new infrared system will provide real estate agents with high-speed point-and-beam communication of a wide range of selling information and listing services.

4. As needed, place your announcement within the context of trends or developments that affect your target audiences.
   This week's conversion is the first to take place among the estimated 25,000 real estate agents who work in the San Francisco Bay area

5. Explain the significance or impact the announcement may have on the audiences of the news organizations that receive the release.
   To ensure maximum security for homeowners, the new keys must be updated daily by agents. The keys can also be deactivated the same day an agent reports their key is missing or stolen.

6. Include appropriate facts, figures, and background information about the project or announcement.
   The Marin Association of REALTORS® was instrumental in negotiating a $4 million, six-year technology upgrade contract on behalf of 6,000 real estate agents Marin, Sonoma, Napa, Mendocino, and Solano counties.
   The agents will have the option of upgrading to either a basic dKEY display key (about the size of a small cell phone) or the more advanced eKEY (a Palm handheld computer). The eKEY will provide real estate agents with the latest information from the Multiple Listing Service, daily updates of housing inventories, and e-mail feedback from other agents about homes on the market. Both devices are provided by GE Interlogix Supra.

7. Be familiar with the news organizations that are important to your organization and when writing the advisory so it addresses their interests and audiences.
   Please contact Edward Segal at 415-507-1011 to schedule a tour of the key conversion process that is taking place this Monday, Tuesday, and Wednesday at the Embassy Suites Hotel at 1101 McInnis Parkway in San Rafael, or to arrange interviews with officials of the Marin Association of REALTORS® which is coordinating this week's technology upgrade

8. Limit the length of the advisory to one single-spaced page.

9. Include the name and phone number for reporters to call if they have questions about the advisory.

For the latest examples of news advisories, click on the "tools of the trade" link on the home page of www.ProfitByPublicity.com. Also, be sure to visit my blog at http://ProfitByPublicity.blogspot.com.

The Bottom Line

- Use a news advisory to invite reporters to attend an event, attend a formal announcement, or news conference.
- Send a news advisory out a few days prior to the event that you want the media to cover.

How to Generate Publicity: Think Outside the Real Estate Pages

Local Realtor Competes In Chicago Marathon
NILES-Ann Gaines, a local realtor with Coldwell Bank Real Estate Specialists in Niles, knows how to get moving—literally! After four months of training and more than one blister, Gaines completed the Chicago Marathon on Oct. 22. Gaines also received pledges from her fellow agents and community members and was able to raise more than $2,000 for Trinity Lutheran School in Berrien Springs, where her three children attend.

Niles Daily Star
Nov. 11, 2006
Niles, MI

Advice and Insights: By thinking of ways to generate news coverage about yourself outside the real estate sections of your paper, you can dramatically increase the chances of getting publicity for yourself or your real estate company.

A case in point is the story above, which appeared as a *sports* story in the agent's local newspaper. By carefully thinking through which activities of your personal or professional life may be newsworthy, it could make sense for you to pitch story ideas to the editors of the sports, travel, business, cooking, art, community, style, hobby, or other sections/departments of your paper.

The more familiar you are with the different sections of your local newspapers and the stories they cover, the more ideas you are likely to come up with that can generate publicity for you or your real estate company.

Chapter 38

Biographical Profiles

I Was Born in a Log Cabin ...

This chapter provides examples of the different kinds of profile stories that news organizations might do about you, the two ways in which most profile stories are alike, and the secret for getting a news outlet to profile you or your company.

Do you yearn to be the subject of a personality profile by your hometown newspaper, a national television network, or an important business or real estate publication?

The secret for making it happen can be boiled down to three words: Don't be shy. After all, if you (or your public relations agency) don't tell news organizations why you'd make an interesting story, who will (except maybe your mother)?

While personality profiles are as different as the people they profile, the stories do share some basic similarities.

- The people are interesting or have unusual or unique backgrounds and accomplishments.

- The individuals have important observations or lessons to share with others.

For example:

Realtor Ranks Surge with New Blood
According to local residential real estate professionals, not only has the hot market attracted new talent to the industry, but it has also attracted more diverse and educated people. John Zeiter, a broker at Platinum Real Estate in San Rafael, embodies this trend. Dissatisfied with his position as an executive vice president at a local manufacturing firm, Mr. Zeiter believed his tech

know-how would translate well to the real-estate industry. So he left this job and established the small brokerage.

North Bay Business Journal
July 18, 2005
Santa Rosa, Calif.

Personality profiles are excellent ways to get the media to highlight an important, interesting, or unusual part of your life, expertise, or accomplishments that can set you apart from other agents or brokers. Here's another example:

Longtime Broker Shuns Retirement, Just Keeps On Selling
The real estate bug bit John Foltz early in life and he really didn't look hard for the cure. Foltz, president and designated broker of Realty Executives in Phoenix, grew up in the small town of Minocqua in northern Wisconsin. He got a taste of the business helping his father sell lake cottages in the scenic area he said was straight out of an old Hamm's beer "land of sky blue waters" ad.

Arizona Republic
March 27, 2005
Phoenix, Ariz.

What's the best story angle or news hook you should use to get the media interested in profiling you or your company? It all depends on you.

If you are young and new to the industry, then the "youth angle" might be your best news hook:

Student Real-Estate Agents Cashing In On Local Market
Between classes at Florida State University, Michael Havens is trying to sell a $589,000 house in northeast Tallahassee. It's not a gimmick. He's not hustling homes on eBay. Havens, 21, is a full-time FSU student and an agent for Volare Real Estate.

Tallahassee Democrat
April 7, 2006
Tallahassee, Fla.

Or it may be that the momentum you've achieved for your new real estate business is the winning ticket:

Young Real Estate Agent Stakes a Claim
After going to school in Colorado and being away from Lafayette for eight years, Jim Keaty decided to return home and start his own real estate firm. Although open less than two years, Keaty Real Estate is already starting to make a name for itself with its blue signs popping up at properties all around town.

The Daily Advertiser
March 19, 2006
Lafayette, La.

Perhaps it's your early interest in real estate:

Max Minzenberger is the kind of guy who is wired to be a salesman. He's personable. He's energetic. He's a self-starter. So it's no surprise that he has found success as a real estate agent. What's interesting about his story is that he knew in college he wanted to pursue a real estate career. And after a brief stint in corporate sales, a 25-year-old Minzenberger left behind a steady salary and appealing benefits package to work as a commission-only agent for Semonin Realtors.

Business First of Louisville
July 2, 2005
Louisville, Ky.

Or, if like most people, you were in a different line of work before you became an agent or broker, perhaps details about your "previous life" will grab the media's attention:

Rocker Takes up Realty
The real estate business attracts people form all walks of life, but it is fair to say there's only one Southwest Florida Realtor who has been knocked out of Billboard's No. 1 spot by The Beatles. Rick Derringer was just 17 when his band, The McCoy's, recorded the No. 1 hit "Hang on Snoopy" in the summer of 1965. Weeks later, the boys from Liverpool nudged out Derringer with the classic "Yesterday." Now Derringer, 58, is working his latest gig—this time as sales agent for Sarasota's McKenna and Associates Realty.

Sarasota Herald-Tribune
June 14, 2006
Sarasota, Fla.

If you've been in the business for a while, then a look back at your successful career might be the story angle that captures the interest of a journalist:

In a previous life, Desiree Callender had a job in hospital administration that was interesting and provided steady income. But she felt it was just a job, not a career. Thirty years later, Callender, now an award-winning Realtor and associate broker, remembers how she tried to figure out what to do.

The Business Gazette
June 17, 2005
Gaithersburg, Md.

Then again, it could be the nature of your clients that makes you interesting to the media:

On Way to Becoming a Teacher, Coralee Barkela Took Successful Detour into Real Estate
In 30 years in real estate, Coralee Barkela has sold homes to and for the rich and famous and sometimes in the infamous: from rock stars, to professional athletes, to well-known business executives and even to a bank robber.

North Bay Business Journal
June 26, 2006
Santa Rosa, Calif.

There are many similarities between pitching a news story to journalists and pitching a profile story. For more information, please see Chapter 20.

For the latest examples of biographical or company profiles, click on the "tools of the trade" link on the home page of www.ProfitByPublicity.com. Also, be sure to visit my blog at http://ProfitByPublicity.blogspot.com.

The Bottom Line

- If you want a news organization to do a profile story about you or your company, don't be shy or coy in pitching the suggestion to editors or reporters.
- The best story angle will depend on the background of you or your company.

How to Generate Publicity: Offer Your Observations about Local Housing Conditions

Real Estate Stalemate
In what real estate professionals are calling a much-needed correction, real estate prices on the Cape have begun falling as sellers try to avoid getting stuck in a glutted market. But although it's clearly a buyer's market, buyers aren't exactly rushing to buy. "The way I think of it is a wait and see market," said Carol Blair, office manager and broker with Coastal Properties in Chattham. "The sellers are not happy about putting their price down because the buyers aren't buying, and the buyers are waiting. It's as if real estate is in a holding pattern."

The Cape Codder
July 21, 2006
Cape Cod, Mass.

Advice and Insights: If you or your real estate company have expertise or specialized knowledge about the local housing market or other real-estate related topics, then your comments, observations, or warnings on these subjects might attract local and even national attention.

Your comments must be warranted, supported by the facts, and not made just for the sake of seeing your name in the newspaper or your face on television. Otherwise, you'll be compared to the story of the boy who cried wolf and your image and reputation will suffer accordingly.

On the other hand, if you have strong opinions or feelings about a real estate topic you think will interest or concern the public, then that publicity can accomplish two goals at once: provide an important public service while legitimately generating public recognition for your expertise.

Chapter 39

Op-Eds and Bylined Articles

Everyone Is Entitled to My Opinion

Here are nine ways to prepare opinion pieces to ensure they are published in newspapers.

Op-eds and bylined articles are opinion pieces published by newspapers and magazines that explain and discuss an individual's viewpoints, observations, or experiences. They are also excellent vehicles for establishing or reinforcing your expertise on a real estate-related topic.

These articles are also an excellent way to promote your name, expertise, and contact information via the media. For example, when REALTOR® Janet Leavitt wrote a bylined article for *San Diego Business Journal* in 2005 about the dangers consumers face when selling their homes without using a REALTOR®, the following copy was included at the end of her piece:

Janet Leavitt [is] a Realtor® with Coldwell Banker Prestige Properties in Escondido, Calif., San Diego County. She is one of only 1,500 Realtors worldwide designated as a Certified International Property Specialist (CIPS) by the National Association of Realtors. Contact her at e-mail: leavise@aol.com, (760) 749-4640, or view her website at www.iloveproperty.biz.

It's important to remember, however, that most local newspapers prefer that submissions be made by people living in their readership area. Also, the space that publications reserve for these articles is quite limited, so you should read several issues of the publication to determine which topics they are most interested in covering, and ask them to send you a copy of their guidelines before you write or submit your article.

Effective Op-Eds

The best op-eds and bylined articles are those that:

1. Provide readers with a new, interesting, or unusual perspective on an issue, cause, or topic.

2. Help to educate or inform the reader about a topic that concerns them.

3. Provide readers with information or lessons they probably would not receive anywhere else.

4. Help to link the topic to local or national events, trends, or developments.

5. Are based on your experience or expertise.

6. Are written to address the needs or concerns of the readers of the publication.

7. Are usually 500 to 1,000 words in length (depends on the publication).

8. Are subject to editing and condensing with or without your approval.

9. Are submitted to one publication at a time for their consideration.

The best way to get an idea about the topics and issues that will make the best subjects for an op-ed or bylined article is simply read through several recent issues of the publication where you'd like to have your article appear, pay close attention to what topics are attracting the attention of other news organizations, or try to get a sense about what the hottest topics may be during the next few days or weeks.

Once you've chosen a topic, however, don't waste any time preparing the article and sending it to the editor; as with everything else, your timing can be crucial. Remember that nothing is as boring as yesterday's news—or opinions.

A sample op-ed that was published on Oct. 30, 2006 by the *Marin Independent Journal* in San Rafael, Calif. follows below.

The Housing Sky Is Not Falling

Recent newspaper headlines such as "housing prices fall" and "housing prices predicted to drop" are—understandably—raising concerns and fears among homeowners and home sellers here and across the country. Unfortunately, these and similar "scary" headlines do not accurately reflect the insights and perspectives of real estate experts, the realities of the marketplace, or the unique nature of Marin.

In short, it's time for a reality check.

It's not as bad as it appears. Although the median price for single family homes in Marin decreased 3.3% from September 2005 to September 2006, the decrease is not significant. Indeed, if you combine condo and single family home sales, the median price actually *increased* by 1.4 % over the year.

You can't judge real estate trends by focusing only on small snapshots of the market. As reported in *Realty Times*, Mike Moran, chief economist for Daiwa Securities America, Inc., says the housing market "is going through a correction that's badly needed" after five years of record sales and price appreciation. "The key issue is whether it is orderly or disorderly"—and it's clearly the former. Yet the financial press and TV news programs are "portraying it as a catastrophe." Other economists agree.

Keep things in perspective. According to Vince Malta, president of the California Association of REALTORS®, "Over the long term, residential real estate in California has been and will continue to be a solid investment. Since 1968, the long-term average price appreciation is 9.1 percent."

Marin is Different. Marin County tends to be more insulated concerning market downturns since we have little new housing or raw, developable land, and have a diversified economic base. Our county is not dominated by one type of industry or even one company.

Balance is Back. Gone are the days of multiple offers and houses lasting a week on the market. We are in a more balanced and healthier market. Both parties to the transaction are negotiating and we see more "win/win" transactions. Due to an increase in supply of homes for sale, buyers can take more time making their purchasing decisions and houses are staying on the market longer.

The Downturn May be Short-lived. The Vice Chairman of the Federal Reserve, Donald L. Kohn, stated in a recent speech that the present downturn in the real estate market may be relatively short-lived. He indicated that new housing "starts may be closer to their [low point] than to their peak." Mid-2005 was the peak of the recent five year housing boom and the opinion of experts is that the correction will be mild and of a short duration.

Buyers, Your Time is Now. Buyers need to wake up and jump in the market now while the real estate market swing is in their favor. Besides the great tax advantages of owning versus renting your home, interest rates are still at historical lows. Also, many homes have been on the market over 90 days and sellers are dropping their prices to attract offers. Lower listing prices will clear out inventory and prices will stabilize.

Consult with local experts who know what they are talking about. Contact a local REALTOR® who has access to the latest facts, figures and trends about the Marin housing market. They are the best individuals to provide you with the important information, insights and perspectives you need to help you make informed and intelligent decisions when you sell or buy a home.

The bottom line is this: When it comes to today's housing market—especially in Marin—the sky is not falling.

Kathy Schlegel is president of the Marin Association of REALTORS® in San Rafael. Visit its Web site at www.MarinCountyRealtors.com.

For the latest examples of op-eds and bylined articles, click on the "tools of the trade" link on the home page of www.ProfitByPublicity.com. Also, be sure to visit my blog at http://ProfitByPublicity.blogspot.com.

The Bottom Line

- Op-eds and bylined articles are opinion pieces published by newspapers and magazines that explain and discuss an individual's viewpoints, observations, or experiences.

- They are also excellent vehicles for establishing or reinforcing your expertise on a real estate-related topic and to promote your name, expertise, and contact information via the media.

How to Generate Publicity: Advocate Affordable Housing

A Huge Boost for Workforce Housing
[Last] week the Marin Workforce Housing Trust was launched with an impressive $500,000 pledge from three Marin businesses [including] Frank Howard Allen Realtors.

Editorial, Marin Independent Journal
June 20, 2004
San Rafael, Calif.

Advice and Insights: The issue of affordable housing is one of the most pressing issues facing many communities. That's because many key members of those communities—including law enforcement officials, teachers, health care professionals and firefighters—often cannot afford to live in those communities.

Given the importance that housing plays in the fabric and economy of communities, it is no wonder that news organizations pay so much attention to various facets of this critical topic.

That attention takes many forms, including newspaper editorials, feature stories on the local television news program, and articles in the daily and weekly newspapers.

Real estate agents and brokers who take a leadership role in addressing the affordable housing situation in their area are often prime candidates for news coverage about those efforts. Their efforts—and yours—may include:

- Spearheading fundraising activities in the community.
- Making a financial contribution to an affordable housing project.
- Testifying in support of a housing initiative when it comes before a planning commission, city council, or other government body.
- Working with corporate and community leaders to help make affordable housing a reality.
- Organizing conferences, summits, or town hall meetings to help educate the public about the problem and possible solutions.
- Launching public awareness campaigns to inform the public about housing programs and the importance of affordable housing initiatives.
- Working with Habitat for Humanity or other such organizations to build houses for deserving families.

Chapter 40

Letters to the Editor

Dear Sir:

Eight ways to help guarantee your letters to newspapers or magazines are published.

Writing letters to the editor is a time-honored way to express views, comment on current events, seek to correct mistakes by the media, and respond to the opinions of editors and readers.

The correspondence is also an easy and affordable way to establish or reinforce your credibility or expertise on an issue while getting free publicity for yourself or your company.

For example:

It's Unfair to Blame Real Estate Agents for High Housing Prices in Region
Homeowners like David Bookbinder ("Brokers helping to drive up Northeast housing prices," Globe North letter, July 16) who have had to carry two mortgages, know all too well that housing demand has slowed, but to point an accusatory finger at "overzealous" brokers as the reason why home prices have risen so sharply in recent years is shortsighted and unfair. In reality, economic principles and local community decision-making are primarily to blame.
(Excerpt from a letter to the editor from Mark Hutchinson Melrose, Northeast region vice president of the Massachusetts Association of REALTORS®)

The Boston Globe
July 23, 2006
Boston, Mass.

Unfortunately, given the volume of mail that newspapers and magazines receive, there is no guarantee that any letter you send will be used. Even if it is selected for publication, it can be edited and condensed without your approval.

Checklist

Follow these suggestions to help ensure that your letter is used and printed the way you wrote it:

- Respond as quickly as possible to the story or event about which you are writing. Check with the publication on how they prefer to receive letters from readers: mail, fax, e-mail, overnight delivery, or even by messenger.

- Keep it short, from 25 to 250 words depending on the publication.

- Remember that whatever you write may be edited or shortened by the editor before it is printed.

- Keep your comments focused on the story or event you are responding to.

- While it can be appropriate to refer to your expertise or experience in the matter, do not turn your letter into a commercial for you or your company.

- Review the letters or comments that appear in recent issues of the publication so you can get a sense about the style, format, length, and content of the letters they publish.

- Before you send your letter, be sure to read it out loud to help you catch any grammatical or other errors.

- Check with the newspaper or magazine for their submission guidelines.

For the latest examples of letters to the editor, click on the "tools of the trade" link on the home page of www.ProfitByPublicity.com. Also, be sure to visit my blog at http://ProfitByPublicity.blogspot.com.

The Bottom Line

- Writing letters to the editor is a time-honored way to express views, comment on current events, seek to correct mistakes by the media, and respond to the opinions of editors and readers.

- The correspondence is also an easy and affordable way to establish or reinforce your credibility or expertise on an issue while getting free publicity for yourself or your company.

How to Generate Publicity: Form Joint Ventures or Alliances

Joint Venture Can Help Home Buyers
Alan Pinel Realtors on Tuesday announced a joint venture with Wells Fargo Home Mortgage aimed at giving potential home buyers all of their real estate and financial needs in one place. The joint venture will be called Private Mortgage Advisors, LLC, and will be present at all 22 Alan Pinel Realtors' offices through out the Bay area, including those in San Mateo, Alameda and Contra Costa counties.

Oakland Tribune
June 9, 2004
Oakland, Calif.

Advice and Insights: Large real estate state companies should carefully examine all of their business activities and decisions for potential news hooks—such as joint ventures—that are beyond the grasp of smaller competitors.

Chapter 41

Video News Releases

Lights, Camera, Action!

How you can generate national publicity by packaging and distributing a self-produced television story.

If you watch the local news on television with any regularity, the chances are pretty good you've seen a video news release and did not realize it.

Video news releases (or VNRs) appear to be just like any one of the hundreds of other news reports you've seen on the television station. They are complete 90-second stories that hundreds of TV stations across the country air in whole or in part during their regular local newscasts.

But there are several important differences between a VNR and other TV news reports:

1. The story is usually about some aspect of the products, services, or activities of a corporation or organization.

2. You probably don't recognize the name of the reporter or have never seen him or her on the air.

3. Every aspect of the story—including research, preparation of the script, and producing and editing the report—was handled not by the news department at the TV station that broadcast the story, but by a private company that produced the VNR.

4. The news report has been paid for by a corporation or organization, usually in order to help publicize the product, service, or activity that was the subject of the video news release.

VNRs are most often used by smaller or mid-sized newsrooms with smaller staffs and limited resources, while bigger newsrooms shoot their own video and tend to rely on stories that are sent to them from the TV networks and satellite news feeds. The larger stations, however, may incorporate portions of a VNR into their stories or delete the reporter who appears on the VNR—and replace them with one of their own.

A VNR can be an important way to help tell your story to television audiences across the country if you have:

- A story that is of interest to millions of people and can be localized for local television audiences.

- Good pictures to help show your story. Remember, this is television, which depends on good pictures.

- Enough money. Typical VNRs can cost several thousands of dollars to produce and distribute.

- Enough time and patience. Allowing for research, script preparation, shooting schedules, and editing time, it can take from several days to several weeks to produce and complete the finished piece.

- In addition to providing you with a polished, broadcast-quality video news report, most VNR production or distribution companies can make arrangements to track the usage of the report; provide you with documentation about which stations aired all or parts of the VNR, when the story was broadcast; and tell you the estimated number of people who saw it. Some firms can also get you copies of the "air checks"—copies of the story as it was seen on each TV station.

As important as VNRs are to help promote corporations and organizations, the videos are also important to the television stations that receive them. That's because the packaged reports serve as an important and free source of news programming for budget-strapped stations that cannot afford the time or staff to produce the same stories on their own, or as a source of story ideas for their own reporters.

Indeed, if properly and effectively done, VNRs have something to offer everyone: news coverage for the companies that sponsor them, an important source of programming for the TV stations that get them, and news for the audiences that watch them.

For the latest examples of VNRs, click on the "tools of the trade" link on the home page of www.ProfitByPublicity.com. Also, be sure to visit my blog at http://ProfitByPublicity.blogspot.com.

VNRs for Radio

An audio news release (ANR) is similar to a video news release, but is produced and distributed for use on radio stations. Instead of pictures, however, the ANR relies on narration and sound bites. The finished piece is nearly identical to a "real" news report you'd hear on your local radio station.

For the latest examples of ANRs, click on the "tools of the trade" link on the home page of www.ProfitByPublicity.com.

Resources

For information about producing and distributing VNRs and ANRs, visit www.medialink.com.

The Bottom Line

- Video news releases appear to be just like any one of the hundreds of other news reports you've seen on television stations.

- They are complete 90-second stories that hundreds of TV stations across the country air in whole or in part during their regular local newscasts.

- VNRs are most often used by smaller or mid-sized newsrooms with smaller staffs and limited resources.

How to Generate Publicity: Comment on Real Estate Trends

Slowing Sales Test Real Estate Agents Locally
"You work longer hours, and you sell less," said [Lynn] Bates, an agent with Century 21 Associates West. "We're finding there are fewer buyers, and the ones that do come in are less committed to the process. Some people will write offers and then change their minds. That's happening a lot more."

San Luis Obispo Tribune
July 23, 2006
San Luis Obispo, Calif.

Advice and Insights: News organization regularly report statistics concerning local and national real estate trends and developments. But journalists often add perspective and commentary to their stories by interviewing agents and brokers for their reactions and observations. If you know what you're talking about, and know how to talk to reporters, speak up and let them know you're available for interviews about local real estate trends.

Chapter 42

News Conferences

Risks and Rewards

The benefits and drawbacks of staging a news conference, and 14 steps you can take to ensure their success.

News conferences can be the easiest and most effective way to meet with and answer the questions of as many reporters as possible at one time about a story or news announcement.

Indeed, the very fact that you've scheduled a news conference can help raise the media's interest in covering your story since they assume you'd schedule the event only if you had important news to discuss.

Of course, depending on the number of news organizations in your area, a news conference may be unnecessary or totally inappropriate. And for the sake of your own credibility with the media, it is absolutely essential that the topic of your news conference is truly newsworthy and deserves the increased attention and scrutiny of journalists.

Unfortunately, news conferences are also one of the riskiest ways to generate news coverage, since any number of late-breaking or more important stories may prevent reporters from attending. And once you have assembled a room full of reporters, the journalists may want to cover a different aspect or angle of the story that you did not consider, or did not want to discuss. For example:

Realtors Give $30,000 for Pitch for School Tax
Realtors and school officials linked the quality of public education and schools to quality of life and property values during a news conference Thursday afternoon. It was called primarily to announce the Rockford Area Association of Realtors' $30,000 donation to the Kids Win Steering Committee, charged with campaigning for a Nov. 7 referendum to maintain the school education

fund tax rate. *But officials were peppered with questions about how referendum funding will be spent and consequences should it fail.* (Italics added for emphasis)

Rockford Register Star
Aug. 11, 2006
Rockford, Ill.

Sometimes events beyond your control can torpedo a news conference that appears to have everything going for it.

A case in point is a news conference that I arranged in Washington, D.C. about an important local transportation project, and which promised to be one of the best-covered news stories that day.

There was every indication that I would have a successful event:

- The Associated Press had listed the conference on its daily calendar of scheduled news events.

- Every major television station in the region had agreed to send a reporter and news crew.

- The two daily newspapers had given me the name of the journalists who would attend.

- Several radio stations promised they would send reporters.

- But when it came time for the news conference to start, none of the reporters who said they'd attend were in the room.

Tragically, earlier that morning a Maryland state trooper had been gunned down during a routine traffic stop, and every news organization in the region was, understandably, covering the story.

While I scrambled to send information about our announcement to the reporters who had been scheduled to attend our event, our efforts were to no avail. The murder of the state trooper was big news for several days, dominating all local news coverage. It was impossible to get the media to focus on anything else.

Sometimes the best way to ensure reporters will attend a news conference is to take the news conference to the reporters.

One of my PR clients was scheduled to unveil a new version of its software at COMDEX, the prestigious computer show in Las Vegas. Working with show officials, I scheduled and promoted a news conference at the COMDEX press center to discuss the software. The event was held in a room adjacent to where reporters picked up press passes, press kits, free food, and wrote their stories.

When I entered the room to begin the press conference, more than a dozen editors and reporters were in their seats, ready to listen to my opening remarks and to ask questions about the announcement.

While it is impossible to guard against the unexpected, there are several steps you can take to ensure that your news conference goes off without a hitch.

- Make sure your topic is interesting and newsworthy enough to warrant a full-scale news conference, and that it concerns a timely topic that will impact a large audience.

- Select a location that is easily accessible by reporters.

- Bring or have access to good visuals, charts, graphs, etc. to show your story or demonstrate your announcement.

- Schedule the conference early in the day: Between 10 AM and Noon is best.

- Shorter is always better: it should not last more than 15 to 20 minutes.

- Have refreshments available for reporters.

- If possible, notify the media about the conference two to three days ahead of time, and call reporters the night before or the morning of the event to remind them.

- Begin the conference with a brief opening statement (three to five minutes), and then spend as much time as possible answering reporters' questions.

- Bring and distribute copies of the opening statement and any appropriate background information (press kits, fact sheets, etc.).

- Check out the site of the news conference several days ahead of time.

- Make sure you have ordered any equipment or supplies you need, and that the equipment is in working order before the start of the news conference.

- Have a sign-in sheet for reporters so you can track attendance.

- If necessary, post signs in building lobbies, hallways, etc. to direct reporters to the site of the news conference.

- Arrive early to ensure that all arrangements are in place and that everything is in working order.

Your News Conference Checklist

Of all the "tools of the trade" you may use to generate news coverage about yourself or your organization, holding a news conference will likely be the one activity that will require the most time, resources, and planning.

To give you a better idea about the work that can be involved and the attention to detail that is required to successfully stage one of these events, following are highlights of the task list I prepared as I worked with the National Park Service to hold a news conference for the Secretary of the Interior.

- Finalize/approve date, time, location, staging, and details of event.
- Finalize/approve target audiences.
- Finalize/approve the geographic focus of the desired news coverage.
- Finalize/approve themes and messages to be communicated to the target audiences.
- Finalize/approve list of participants and speakers.
- Prepare draft press materials, including news advisory, news release, fact sheet, and press kit.
- Draft suggested sound bites for participants.
- Research/obtain media lists.
- Script event (who will say what, where they will stand, etc.).
- Issue invitations to participants and speakers.
- Approve all press kit materials.
- Distribute news advisory via mail and fax.
- Distribute news release via US Newswire.
- Post news advisory on agency's Web site.
- Finalize/approve draft press materials.
- Finalize/approve sound bites.
- Finalize/approve script of event.
- Prepare/finalize remarks for participants.
- Confirm attendance of invited participants.
- Obtain copies of remarks to be made by speakers.
- Place follow-up calls to selected editors and reporters to encourage them to attend.
- Retain print and TV media monitoring services.

- Retain local photographer to document event.
- Produce/assemble press kits.
- Confirm that event is listed on wire service daybooks and TV and newspaper listings of scheduled news events.
- Visit site of news conference.
- Confirm physical arrangements (podium, PA system, signage, etc.).
- Finalize staging and visuals.
- Conduct walk-through of event with participants or their representatives.
- Deliver all press materials, charts, graphs, etc. to local hotel.
- Place reminder calls to key news organizations about the event.
- Arrive at least two hours early to set up site.
- Hold news conference.
- Distribute press materials to media at event.
- Distribute news release via e-mail, mail and fax immediately after the event.
- Distribute news release via US Newswire.
- Seek to arrange press interviews with agency and National Park Service officials.
- Post news release and fact sheet on agency's Web site.

Depending on your news announcement, it may make more sense for you to stage a photo op, which is arranged for the benefit of television cameras and photographers. Here, visuals are essential, so make sure you have a story—and the pictures to go along with it—that will make the event worthwhile for you and the media.

A New Wrinkle

Thanks to the Internet, it's now possible to stage a successful news conference without having a single reporter show up. By holding an "e-conference" at your Web site, you can invite and have any number of reporters and editors see and hear the event; show a video, slides, or other graphics to help illustrate your points; and allow reporters to ask questions via their computer keyboards and receive all the information they need to file stories about your news conference.

The Bottom Line

- News conferences can be the most effective—yet riskiest—way to generate news coverage about an important announcement or story.

How to Generate Publicity: Market Yourself in Creative Ways

Real Estate Agents Are Finding Creative Ways to Stand Out From the Competition
In the ongoing battle for name recognition, Spring Cho recently unveiled her latest weapon: a chic new graphic with the real estate agent's headshot rendered in simple black strokes a la Andy Warhol, silk-screen style.

The Roanoke Times
June 29, 2006
Roanoke, Va.

Advice and Insights: What's the big deal? Many real estate agents use a headshot on their business cards. But how many of them use the photos in a creative or unusual way?

When they do, it can be big deal—at least to some reporters.

Chapter 43

Satellite Media Tours

How to Be in Two Places at Once

Practical advice on when and why you may want to use satellite technology to help spread the word about yourself or your company.

Thanks to satellite media tours (SMTs), it's possible for you to be interviewed by television reporters in scores of different cities across the country on the same day without having to get on an airplane.

A SMT is a series of one-on-one interviews with television reporters or the anchors of a news show either for live broadcast or later use in a news story.

While you sit in the comfort of a television studio or remote location, technicians bring online journalists who had previously agreed to participate in the tour and to interview you for a few minutes.

Depending on the topic and the interest among television stations, it's possible for you to be interviewed by as many as 20 stations within the course of three hours. Before you even think about a SMT, however, it is important to have a story or announcement that will likely attract a national audience.

Of course, given the costs to produce a SMT (which can run into several thousands of dollars), this PR tactic is something only a large regional or national real estate company will have the need, interest, or financial resources to do.

Resources

For more information on SMTs, visit www.medialink.com.

The Bottom Line

- Satellite media tours enable you to appear in several cities on the same day without traveling.
- They are expensive to do and you should only consider doing them if you have an important or major regional or national story to discuss.

How to Generate Publicity: Promote Your Listings in Unusual Ways

Realtors Let House Do the Talking

With so many houses on the market, Valley Realtors are trying hard to make their listings special. Adam Hamblen thinks he's found a way. "Ours is the one with the talking house, and that's what makes ours stand out," he said. The house itself doesn't talk. Rather, Hamblen's business partner, Dave Kinnaman, does the talking, with the help of a transmitter.

"They give you some suggested dialogue you can do and we kind of fill in with information about the property," said Hamblen, an agent with RES and Associates. Potential buyers driving by the pair's eight current listings will notice extra signs in the yard. They read "Talking House," with instructions to tune to a designated AM radio frequency.

Arizona Republic
Nov. 2, 2006
Phoenix, Ariz.

Advice and Insights: Never underestimate the media's interest in doing stories about the new tools—or toys—real estate agents use to help market their listings.

Chapter 44

Finding and Contacting the Reporters

How to Reach the Right People

Eight ways to ensure you send press materials to the journalists who will be most interested in receiving them.

Over the years, I've generated as much news coverage for my PR clients and the Marin Association of REALTORS® from reporters I did not know as from journalists with whom I've had long working relationships. That's because a good story can be like bait: it can encourage reporters to come to you—whether you know them or not.

Indeed, when I was the marketing strategies columnist for *The Wall Street Journal's* StartupJournal.com, I had no qualms about dealing with complete strangers who wanted to be in my columns—as long as they had a good story to tell and the right credentials. As a freelance writer, I often use a service such as Profnet.com, which helps make it possible for reporters to find experts or sources they can interview for their articles.

Since most local news organizations usually assign the task of covering real estate stories to one reporter, it is relatively easy to track that person down so you can pitch your story directly to him or her.

- Simply call the paper and ask the operator for the name and phone number or e-mail of their real estate or business reporter, or the columnist you think will be most interested in your story or announcement.

- Some newspapers list the phone number or e-mail of their reporters with the stories they write.

- When seeking television or radio coverage for your story, call the local stations and ask to speak to their news assignment editor.

- It can be helpful to both you and the reporter if you get to know the journalist before you have a story to pitch them. The sooner you get to know them, the sooner you'll know what specific real estate stories they may be interested in covering. The reporter will get a better idea about your own areas of real estate expertise. This may in turn suggest news hooks and story angles that may be of interest to the reporter and his audience.

- If you want news organizations to cover a special event or news conference, it will also help to call the local office of the Associated Press and ask them to list your event on their daybook (or calendar) of scheduled events and activities.

But if it's important that you notify as many news organizations as possible about your news or event, there are several services that can help you get the job done, such as:

- Private news wire services (see resources section below) who, for a fee, will send your release electronically to the different categories of news organizations you specify, or nationwide to thousands of editors and reporters.

Whichever way you decide to go, keep the following advice in mind:

- Since the features and costs for these and other services are always subject to change, be sure to contact them or their Web sites for the latest and most up-to-date information, and cost-compare to decide which is best for you based on your needs and budget.

- Use a heavy dose of common sense in determining how much time, effort and money to spend in distributing your news release. If you send releases to people who common sense would tell you have absolutely no interest in reading them, then you are wasting both your time and theirs. And remember that different reporters have different preferences for how they like to receive information—phone, fax, e-mail, or snail mail.

If, as part of your marketing activities, you send a real estate newsletter to clients and new business prospects, then you've left off an important audience from the distribution list: the media.

Most editors, reporters, and columnists are always on the lookout for new story leads, article ideas, and reliable sources of information about the topics and issues they cover.

Real estate-related stories are no exception.

That's why it makes sense to send a copy of your latest printed or e-mail newsletter to the journalists who cover real estate in your area, have done stories about you in the past, or who you'd like to write about you in the future.

Sending newsletters to the media is also a good way to get "more bang for the buck" out of the work you put into the newsletter in the first place.

- The information in your newsletter may be perceived by reporters as being less intrusive than sending story pitch letters or "pestering" them with story ideas over the telephone.

- Post the newsletter on your Web site, as well as an archive of past issues— but only if you are willing to share the contents with the rest of the world.

- Carefully review your publication to determine whether its content will be of interest to journalists in the first place.

- If you have any doubts whether reporters would be interested in receiving your newsletter, just ask them. And always remove them promptly from the distribution list if they say they want to stop receiving them.

Resources

Visit the following Web sites for information about services that will distribute your news release to editors and reporters:

- www.prnewswire.com.
- www.businesswire.com.

The Bottom Line

- Depending on your media market, it may be impossible to know all the reporters who may be interested in doing stories about you or your real estate company.

- Take steps to make sure reporters know about you and how to reach you for their stories.

How to Generate Publicity: Join an Organization

Peter Richmond, an agent with Pacific Union Real Estate Group, Ltd. of Mill Valley, was among a select group of real estate professionals across the country accepted into Cyberstars, a national technology organization.

Marin Independent Journal
Jan. 28, 2004
San Rafael, Calif.

Advice and Insights: This brief newspaper story was published on the front page of the financial section in their "business briefs" column. Many daily and weekly papers have similar features in their own financial pages—features that require a steady stream of stories to fill on a regular basis. Because of the need to fill this void, even the most mundane activities—such as joining an organization—may result in publicity for you or your real estate company.

Chapter 45

Story Pitch Calls, E-mails, and Letters

Other Ways to Grab the Media's Attention

This chapter explains other effective ways to promote your story idea to reporters.

As important as news releases are to tell your story to the media (see Chapter 34), some people are more comfortable sending a letter or making a phone call to editors and reporters instead. And sometimes the relatively dry aspects of the who, what, when, where, why, and how of a traditional news release may not do justice to the drama, action, emotion, or unusual human interest angle of your story.

In these instances, consider calling or sending a story pitch letter or e-mail.

These brief e-mail messages, letters, or phone calls to journalists explain the importance or significance of news hooks, story angle, an announcement, or event, and encourage the reporters to do stories about them.

Following are excerpts from an exchange of e-mails between a reporter and Sperry Van Ness (a national commercial real estate brokerage in Irvine, Calif.), which was trying to pitch a story to a business reporter about property trends in the Koreatown section of Los Angeles.

Sperry Van Ness: Are you ever looking for story/trend ideas? I have an idea that you may be interested in.

Reporter: I'm backlogged with stories I want to do right now. But I'm always open to story ideas. So send it on over.

Sperry Van Ness: Have you guys ever considered doing a story on the Koreatown multifamily market? Here are some facts to consider though, I am still trying to get more specifics for you. The rents and property values in Koreatown have had the largest change of dramatic appreciation in Los Angeles over the past few years. Koreatown has seen a huge run-up in sales prices as major investment players from other markets have been targeting it.

Reporter: That does sound interesting. As you learn more shoot it to me.

Sperry Van Ness: Sorry to bother but I was just curious if you have had a chance to consider writing a story on the Koreatown multifamily market. If you are interested I can definitely get you in touch with our top broker in that area who could provide more insight. I'm sure he'd be more than happy to give you a tour of the area if you want. Please help me know how I can help.

Reporter: Sorry it took me so long to get back to you. It's definitely interesting. I would have to have comparative figures from other submarkets in order to know if the Koreatown submarket is truly exceptional for Los Angeles. If they aren't, I will probably just watch to see if it stays strong when the rest of the market slows.

Reporter: Do you still have the stats you sent me before comparing West Los Angeles, Santa Monica and Koreatown? I just realized the Excel file you sent only had West LA and Santa Monica stats and not Koreatown.

Sperry Van Ness: Sorry for the delay in getting back to you. Here are some comparative figures for Santa Monica and West Los Angeles that clearly shows that Koreatown has truly been the premier multifamily submarket in Los Angeles. As you will see, median price per unit increased by 100 percent in Koreatown over the past 5 years as compared to an 83 percent increase in West Los Angeles and a 64 percent increase in Santa Monica. The 10 year increase is much greater with Koreatown coming in at 451 percent compared to 324 percent in West Los Angeles and 294 percent in Santa Monica. Please let me know if this helps.

The story pitch was successful, and resulted in a full-page article that included a photo of a Sperry Van Ness agent standing in front of a property he had sold in Koreatown.

The Bottom Line

- Sometimes it makes sense to pitch a story idea to a reporter even before you send them a news release about your story.

- These brief e-mail messages, letters, or phone calls to journalists explain the importance or significance of news hooks, story angles, announcements, or events, and encourage the reporters to do stories about them.

How to Generate Publicity: Put a New Twist on Marketing Efforts

Real Estate Agents Offer New Marketing Strategy
Realtors using value range marketing say it's an unusual, new and foreign concept, but in the much slower real estate market, if it brings in buyers it's worth a try. With value range marketing, or VRM, properties have one list price but are marketed within a price range. Jess Eberhart, an agent with 30A Realty, and David Properties' agent Todd Sachs have co-listed a property using VRM. "The whole idea in showing a range encourages buyers to step forward," Eberhart said.

The Walton Sun
Oct. 6, 2006
Santa Rosa Beach, Fla.

Advice and Insights: Elsewhere in this book you'll find examples of the different tactics agents and brokers have used to promote themselves or their properties. But the story above is a new wrinkle—generating publicity based on the strategy you use to price a property. What will they think of next?

Chapter 46

Serve as a Spokesperson

According to ...

How speaking on behalf of your real estate company can also generate publicity for you.

Each year thousands of individuals across the country are interviewed by news organizations not because of who they are but because of what they do. They are the spokespersons for the corporations or organizations where they work and are the principal liaison between their employer and the media. For example:

> Among the more optimistic real estate watchers is Mike Mayo, a spokesman for the Pinellas Realtor Organization. He points out that Pinellas condos rose in value the past year despite a glut of units. "You don't want to create a panic. We've got enough to deal with what's going on with the property insurance market," Mayo said. "We're not seeing the bubble busting.

St. Petersburg Times
Aug. 19, 2006
St. Petersburg, Fla.

A corporate spokesperson can command the instant attention of an editor or reporter when they call, and are often the first people journalists contact for information or a quote on a story involving the spokesperson's company or organization.

Serving as a spokesperson for your real estate company can be an important and sensitive job, since everything the public knows or believes about your company's services, expertise, opinions, and accomplishments can hinge on your ability to faithfully and accurately convey information to the media and maintain good working relationships with reporters.

Burke Stinson, former spokesperson for AT&T, says "being a spokesperson is much like singing. Everyone can do it, but few do it well." So few, in fact, that he estimates that less than 25 percent of all companies have people in those positions who can represent them effectively to the media.

Who makes the best spokesperson? It depends.

Whether you are the best person to serve as the spokesperson can depend on the size and structure of your real estate company and your background and experience in dealing with the media.

In smaller real estate companies, the typical spokesperson is usually the broker or owner of the company.

At larger companies, the spokesperson may be a senior-ranking real estate agent, broker, or an individual specifically hired to serve as the liaison with the media. A hired spokesperson will likely have had previous experience as a working journalist or press secretary for a politician or other public official.

To be effective and credible in their role, the person who represents the company to the media should:

1. Have the full trust, faith, and confidence of senior corporate officials.

2. Be "in the loop" to receive the information they need to do their job and to have an early "heads-up" of any potential issues or problems that may affect the company's reputation or bottom line.

3. Is a part of the decision-making process for the approval of press materials and statements to the media.

4. Has the resources and technology necessary to do the job, from monitoring the news to distributing press materials.

5. Is guaranteed immediate access to the people he or she needs to answer questions from the media.

The Bottom Line

- Serving as a spokesman for your real estate company is a good way to help generate publicity about yourself.

- Being a spokesman requires essential skills and abilities for dealing with the media.

How to Generate Publicity: Make a Big Deal about Your Big Deals

A Family Tradition Yields $5.4 Billion Coup

Darcy Stacom has worked on many notable transactions in her lengthy career as a commercial real estate broker, but nothing compares to the deal she completed last month—anywhere.

In a span about 10 weeks, Ms. Stacom helped to sell all 110 apartment buildings at Stuyvesant Town and Peter Cooper Village, an 80-acre property along the East River in Manhattan, for a record-breaking price of $5.4 billion. Ms. Stacom— dubbed "Queen of the Skyscrapers" by some in the industry—spent many years preparing her team for such a large transaction. In 2005 alone, she led the sale of more than $7.1 billion worth of real estate, which earned her the title of No. 1 Broker in the World at CB Richard Ellis, a Company awarded to the broker who brings in the most revenue.

The New York Times
Nov. 5, 2006
New York, New York

Advice and Insights: Okay, let's admit it: Multi-billion dollar real estate deals are far and few between and residential real estate agents can only dream about such transactions. But just because your deals are small doesn't mean you can't think big. It never hurts to tell local real estate reporters about deals that may be large or unusual for your area, or involve interesting or unusual properties.

Chapter 47

Newsletters and Web Sites

All Your News That's Fit to Publicize

Six ways to generate publicity in frequently overlooked news outlets.

Because people get their news from so many different sources today, it is important not to overlook any news outlet in your quest to generate news coverage for yourself or your real estate company.

That's why having information from your news releases included in the newsletters and Web sites that are read by members of your target audiences (see Chapter 7) can be just as important as having your announcement covered by other news outlets.

By and large, the strategy for getting newsletters and Web sites to write about you is the same as for other news organizations:

1. Do your research to determine the readership and topics they cover.

2. Read back issues to get a good feel about writing style, editorial preference, etc.

3. Customize the information you send them to the particular interests or concerns of their subscribers.

4. Find out and adhere to their deadline for the submission of news releases and story ideas.

5. If you have any questions or doubts about the kinds of stories they are interested in covering, don't hesitate to call the staff to find out for sure.

6. Keep it short. Their stories are often much shorter than articles in any other kind of publication. Depending on their format, style, and topics covered, the length of most articles may be in the 50 to 200 word range.

So as you seek to generate publicity about yourself or your real estate company, don't forget this important category of news outlets—or the people who read them.

The Bottom Line

- Don't overlook any news outlet in your quest to generate news coverage for yourself or your real estate company.

How to Generate Publicity: Close Deals Quickly

Real Estate Newsmakers
Realtors at the Jack Conway & Co. Dartmouth office bucked the slow real estate market over the Labor Day weekend by selling a house in only three days. Conway Dartmouth agent Janice Hathaway represented the seller and agent Judeth Sullivan represented the buyer, who was coming to Dartmouth from Florida and was referred to the Jack Conway Company from a previous client.

The Standard-Times
Nov. 3, 2006
New Bedford, Mass.

Advice and Insights: You may have heard about speed dating, speed golfing, and speed shopping. Now comes speed real estate. Closing deals so quickly, especially in a slowing real housing market, can definitely be newsworthy. If it happens to you or your company, let local real estate reporters know ASAP.

Chapter 48

Editorial Calendars

Your Own Crystal Ball

How to find out when and where the media will do stories about real estate-related topics.

Wouldn't it be wonderful if you could find out in advance when a newspaper or magazine was planning to run a story, special issue, or supplement about real estate-related topics in your area?

Armed with that information, you could then:

- Decide whether being included in that story would be a good fit with your own efforts to publicize yourself or your real estate company.

- Contact the appropriate editor or reporter to let them know about your interest and availability in being interviewed for their story.

- Offer to provide them with a copy of your news releases or other background information they may need for their article.

- Seek to arrange to be interviewed by the reporter for their story.

All that information and more is available in the form of so-called "editorial calendars" that thousands of news organizations post on their Web sites or will send to you on request.

The calendars, which are used to help sell advertising in that particular issue, include such details as a brief description of the story opportunity; when the article is scheduled to run; how much lead time you have; name, contact, and Web site information; and an overview of the publication.

The two easiest ways to obtain this information are to either pick up your phone or surf the Internet.

1. If you already know which publications you'd like to be quoted in, then it is a simple matter of calling the news organizations and asking them to send you a copy of their editorial calendar.

2. If you want to cast a wider net for story opportunities, simply enter the words "editorial calendar" on your favorite Web site search engine, then click your way through the results.

Resources

For information about editorial calendar search services, please go to www.mediacalendars.com.

The Bottom Line

- Editorial calendars can tell you when a newspaper or magazine in your area is planning on publishing real estate stories or feature articles.

How to Generate Publicity: Hold a Grand Opening

RE/MAX Realty Holds Grand Opening
Georgetown residents George and Janet Hilton, owners of the new RE/MAX Country Crossroads Realty Associates LLC in Rowley, will hold their grand opening Thursday, Nov. 9, 4:30-7:30 PM. The new office is equipped with advanced technology and communication systems available to realtors to better serve the home buyers and home sellers within Rowley and the Essex County communities. Located at 144 Newburyport Turnpike, Suite A8, and surrounded by horse country, the Hiltons' office theme of a "Horse and Hounds Fox Hunt" is a reflection of its name.

Georgetown Record
Nov. 2, 2006
Georgetown, Mass.

Advice and Insights: Grand opening events are not just for supermarkets, hotels, or shopping centers. By a holding an event to promote the opening of a new office, you may also get an opportunity to publicize your address and real estate services or specialties.

Part V

How to Get the Most Out of Your Publicity

19 Ways to Ensure That the Publicity You Receive Continues To Work for You

If you think the impact of the publicity you receive about yourself or your real estate company evaporates the day after it appears, then think again.

News Coverage

For every story you place about your expertise, opinions, activities, or accomplishments, you'll have three important opportunities to get as much mileage out of it as possible: before, during and after the story is published, broadcast, or posted online.

Before

- Send e-mails to your marketing list of clients, co-workers, friends and family members to give them a heads-up with the details of when and where the story is scheduled to appear.

During

- For print and online stories, confirm to the contacts on your marketing list via e-mail or phone calls the fact that the story was published, and tell them how they can read or see it that day.

After

- As part of your ongoing marketing activities, and for those who might have missed the story when it came out, post it on your Web site or blog, include the story (or relevant excerpts) in your listing presentations, or mail a copy to your contacts.

- For radio and television stories, make arrangements for visitors to your Web site to see it via streaming video or hear it through podcast technology.

- Include appropriate portions of the news coverage in your online or printed press kits, newsletters, brochures, and other marketing materials.

News Releases (See Chapter 34)

- Post it on your Web site.
- Post it on your blog.
- Use it as a basis for a podcast.

- Send it via e-mail to your marketing list.
- If the topic of the release is appropriate, include a copy in your presentation listings and other marketing materials.

Articles and Op-eds (See Chapter 39)

Include copies of any article you write:

- On your Web site.
- In your listing presentation and other marketing materials.
- In mailings to clients or prospects.

Internet (See Chapter 33)

- Ask groups and organizations in the community to post links on their Web sites to your home page, blogs, or podcasts.
- Include printed copies of your Web's home page and interesting blog postings in your printed press kit, listing presentation, or other marketing materials.

Speeches (See Chapter 17)

- Post printed excerpts of the speeches you make to groups or organizations on your Web site or blog, and include in your listing presentations and other marketing materials.
- Audiotape or videotape your remarks and post to your Web site using podcast technology, then encourage people to go to your site to listen or watch your speech.

Sponsorships (See Chapter 11)

- Include a list of events, projects, or activities you've sponsored on your Web site, and in your listing presentation and other marketing materials.

Community Involvement, etc. (See Chapter 11)

- List the groups and organizations you belong to, any leadership positions you hold or have held, or any awards or professional recognition you've received on your Web site and in your listing presentation and other marketing information.

How Your Quotes Can Live Forever

Much like the Energizer bunny, thanks to modern technology it's possible for a story about you to keep "going and going and going" long after you've generated publicity about yourself or your company.

That's because almost every story that will ever be written about you may be available to everyone with access to the Internet.

This includes editors, reporters, and columnists who are working on or researching a real estate-related story in which you were quoted. They can, with a few strokes of the computer keyboard, access various computer databases to find those stories or references about you.

And once they find your quote or pithy observation, the journalists can recycle them for use in their own article, or track you down for your latest comments or observations on the subject.

The Bottom Line

- The impact of a story about you or your real estate company does not have to end after the story appears.

- There are many ways to get as much mileage out of your publicity before, during, and after the story is published, broadcast, or posted online.

How to Generate Publicity: Be Creative in How You Market Properties

Real Estate Agents Get Creative
Garden Grove real estate agent Kathy Ladd wasn't going to take the current hous-ing slump lying down. Last month, she printed up 10,000 fliers, recruited Pacifica High cheerleaders to distribute them, rented a bus and held the first "Eastgate & Garden Park Tour of Homes." From 10 AM to 4 PM, buyers were invited to tour 12 open houses, eat barbecue and enter to win a flat-screen TV.

"Day in, day out, we hear bad news. We're doing something about it. [We're] say-ing, 'Here we are. Buy our houses,' said Ladd's assistant, Amber Clausi. "We're trying to let sellers know that we're doing something to drum up business." With Orange County home sales at their lowest level in a decade and buyers facing a staggering glut of listings to choose from, a few agents are getting creative to get their properties noticed.

The Orange County Register
Oct. 13, 2006
Santa Ana, Calif.

Advice and Insights: While it is important for every real estate agent to market their properties, its how the listings are marketed that can result in publicity for the agent. As the story above shows, you don't have to invent a new way to pro-mote listings in order to generate publicity. In this case, the agent combined what others likely have done before: renting a bus, borrowing some local cheerleaders, printing flyers, bringing in food, donating a prize, and coming up with a theme for the event. The combination worked and proved to be a successful recipe for generating publicity.

Glossary

Audio News Releases

The audio version of a video news release (see below), which is sent to the news directors of radio stations to air on news broadcasts.

Biographical Profiles

Provides editors and reporters with key background information about an individual.

Blog

According to Webopedia.com, a blog (short for Weblog) is "a Web page that serves as a publicly accessible personal journal for an individual. Typically updated daily, blogs often reflect the personality of the author." At the time of this writing, blogs were being increasingly embraced by real estate agents, brokers, corporations, and organizations as another way to communicate with their clients, customers, and other target audiences.

Fact Sheets

Provides essential, complex, or detailed background information reporters may need in order to fully understand or accurately report an event or news announcement. May include information that is too long to put into a news release.

Interviews

Opportunities for editors and reporters to talk directly with people who are the subject of news releases or who are making news for some reason. Comments made during interviews are often used as quotes or background information in news reports and articles.

Letters to the Editor

Usually written by readers in response to a story published in a newspaper or magazine about events or developments in the news.

Media Events

Staged events or activities that are designed to provide a backdrop or news hook for news announcement.

Media Kits (aka Press Kits)

A complete package of information that provides the media with everything they need to know about a news announcement. The kit often includes photos, fact sheets, news releases, and related news clippings. Media or press kits can be printed or posted on an organization's Web site.

Media Monitoring Services

Commercial services that monitor newspapers, radio stations, magazines, television news programs, and Web sites for stories that include specified key words. Copies of the news coverage can be used in press kits to provide additional background information to editors and reporters, measure the effectiveness of a public relations campaign, and demonstrate to the media that a story is newsworthy.

Media Training

Professional advice and mock interview sessions which prepare individuals to deal with editors and reporters in a variety of situations and with confidence and authority. The training includes how to ensure that your themes and messages are reported by the media, how to conduct news interviews, how to prepare and use sound bites/ink bites, what to wear and how to stand or sit during interviews, how to handle negative questions, etc.

News Advisories

Serves as a notice or invitation to the media about a planned event, activity, or scheduled news announcement.

News Conferences

A gathering of reporters which enables a newsmaker to meet with as many members of the media as possible at one time and in one place. These events include an opening statement, the distribution of a news release or other press materials, and a question-and-answer period.

News Hook

The basic element of news behind an announcement, activity, or project which will convince editors, reporters, or columnists to do stories about it. The most effective news hooks are those that affect the most people, impact a news organization's audience, and address the audience's interests, needs, or concerns. News hooks vary depending on the nature, needs, and audience of each news organization. The best news hooks answer the question of "who cares?" in a direct, forceful, timely, and compelling manner.

News Releases

The cornerstone of most public relations efforts, these one- to two-page documents explain the who, what, when, where, why, and how of a news announceme

Op-Eds and Bylined Articles

Opinion pieces published by newspapers, magazines, and Web sites which explain and discuss personal viewpoints, observations, or experiences.

Opinion Polls

An effort to determine what the public thinks or feels about an issue or topic. The results of the poll can be used as a news hook to help generate media coverage about a project or cause.

Photo Ops

A step below a formal news conference, photo ops are events which are usually staged for the benefit of television cameras and photographers.

Photos and Cut Lines

Black-and-white or color photos of a person, product, or event, accompanied by a caption which identifies or explains the picture.

Podcasts

Similar to short brief radio programs, they are meant to be listened to on a computer or MP3 player. At the time of this writing, a growing number of corporations and organizations were using podcasts to provide information, advice, and opinions to customers, clients, and other target audiences.

Press Lists

A compilation of editors, reporters, and news organizations that are most likely to be interested in doing a story about an individual, corporation, or organization. The contact information often contains e-mail addresses, phone numbers, fax numbers, and/or mailing addresses.

Resource to the Media

Establishing and maintaining ongoing working relationships with editors and reporters who cover topics or activities in which an individual or company has knowledge, experience, or expertise. By providing them with good quotes and worthwhile story ideas, journalists may come to rely on the individual or company as a source of information for other stories and interview them for those articles or news reports.

Satellite Media Tours

The use of video and satellite technology to enable newsmakers to be interviewed in a short time frame by reporters in different cities across the country within a few minutes or hours.

Sound Bites/Ink Bites

The seven seconds or handful of words excerpted from an interview that may be used in newspaper, radio, television, or wires service stories; the amount of time it takes to read this sentence aloud.

Story Pitch Letters

Brief e-mails or letters to editors and reporters that explain the importance or significance of an announcement or event, and encourages them to do stories about it.

Video News Releases

A complete 90-second news report about an event, activity, or news announcement that is sent to television stations which broadcast local news programs. According to surveys, 75 percent of all television stations accept and use video news releases in some way.

Visuals

The pictures or actions symbolizing the news hooks that will most likely capture the attention of newspaper or magazine photographers and television camera crews.

Profit by Publicity Workshops
for Real Estate Agents and Brokers
Conducted by Edward Segal

- Sharpen your media interview skills
- Prepare and deliver effective speeches and presentations
- Learn from the successes—and mistakes—of others

Edward Segal's workshops are customized to meet the unique need and circumstances of real estate agents, brokers, and REALTOR® associations.

About Edward Segal

- Chief executive officer of the Marin Association of REALTORS®, where he's generated hundreds of stories in the local, state, national, and international media about the activities and accomplishments of the California-based organization.
- A popular speaker who conducts PR workshops for the National Association of REALTORS®, California Association of REALTORS®, local REALTOR® associations, and real estate brokers.
- Former marketing strategies columnist for *The Wall Street Journal's* StartupJournal.com, journalist, PR advisor to more than 500 corporations and organizations, company spokesperson, and press secretary to members of Congress.

Schedule a workshop or keynote speech TODAY for your real agents, brokers, or members
Contact Edward Segal at 415-507-1011 or
Edwards@MarinCountyRealtors.com

Index